By the Waters of Naturalism:

Theology Perplexed Among the Sciences

Andrew P. Porter

Wipf and Stock Publishers
150 West Broadway • Eugene OR 97401
2001

By the Waters of Naturalism
Theology Perplexed Among the Sciences

By Porter, Andrew P.
Copyright©2001 by Porter, Andrew P.
ISBN: 1-57910-770-2

Printed by *Wipf and Stock Publishers*
150 West Broadway • Eugene OR 97401

For the folks in Livermore

Contents

Acknowledgements

Many people have contributed ideas for this book. Edward Hobbs's theology appears on nearly every page, and the few citations don't do him justice. Ed Beutner and Shirley Woods read early drafts and offered encouragement without which the project might well not have gone very far. Mark Richardson, as always, was a sparring partner who contributed more than he knew. I am indebted to Bob Russell for his paper on acts of God, and for the discussion in the Friday Seminar, reading Arthur Peacocke's work on theology and science, during which the key ideas for this book surfaced in my disorderly mind. And to Durwood Foster, for his probing questions during that seminar. Gregory Rocca, OP, and Michael Dodds, OP, read the manuscript and made invaluable criticisms. Without a survey from the Board of Directors of the Fannie and John Hertz Foundation, to which I made impertinent reply, I'm not sure when I would have tumbled to the seven lessons of the Exodus. Without the table fellowship of Rob Fox, Ed Beutner, Denis Roby, and Jerry Ball, I would never have known about Darmok at Tanagra. Without the friendship of Alec Blair, I never would have asked.

This book was typeset in Times Roman with TEX and LATEX macros, on a Intel-box running Debian GNU Linux.

Introduction

In popular culture science seems to be the central challenge to biblical religion and its theology today, and discussions about science and theology inevitably come to the issue of theological naturalism. This perception is not wrong, but seeing how it is right takes some digging. In theologians' experience, the central challenges came not from science but from history, and only a little of that story can be told here. Yet the popular perception is onto something: naturalistic thinking is the major alternative to biblical religion. And people instinctively approach most questions with naturalistic assumptions, even when they think about biblical religion. Unraveling some of those assumptions and looking for alternatives is what this book is about.

Naturalism in theology is the attempt to describe everything that really matters in terms of ideas taken from the natural sciences. But naturalism would be an odd theological method for a historical religion, and biblical religion in all its original forms is supposedly a historical religion. Indeed, one might well ask of science-and-religion conversations, science and *which* religion? If the religion in question is a historical religion, then it might help to look at how historical concepts work.

The idea of action, whether human or divine, seems to be the crossroads through which all these explorations must pass. It is the place to begin. We often think we can see actions (human and divine alike) in the terms of the sciences, physics notable among them. Recent versions of this approach are variants on the god-of-the-gaps theologies, but the older versions, reliant on "miracles," are classic and work in much the same way. Naturalistic ideas about divine action get into trouble fast when you look at them carefully. If historical thinking is instead taken as the guide, religion begins to make sense.

So after we see how naturalistic ideas really don't work well to make sense of biblical religion (chapters 1 and 2), then we can begin to find alternatives (chapters 3 and 4).

The problem of history brings chills and anxieties and uncertainty for biblical religion. Can we know enough? And can we be responsible? Yes, in a word; but that takes some showing (chapter 5).

It will help to have a brief retelling of how it all got started (chapter 6). Without the story of the Exodus, historical religion won't make much sense.

Mircea Eliade once characterized life in history as terror, and so we need to look at how something as precarious as history could ever end in Easter joy (chapter 7). The language we use to speak about these things is analogical (chapter 8), and that's not as strange as it might look. In the end, you have a responsible liberty of interpretation in how you want to conduct a covenant in history (chapter 9), if that doesn't cause too much anxiety.

Chapter 1

Finding God in Physics

1.1 Dilemma

It appears we have to choose between science and religion today—and the only kind of "religion" is Christianity (or Judaism, but Judaism is not much different), and science is not a religion at all. Or that is how things appear. To believe in God means to believe in some kind of a supernatural. Whether or not there is a supernatural today, "religion" says there was one at some times in the past. And if you are religious, you have to give up at least some scientific ideas, because science and religion conflict; science does not allow belief in any kind of supernatural. If you believe in science, then the natural world is all there is, there "is no God", and so making sense of human life must proceed with reference to nature alone. The basic shape of the difficulty is clear: the choice is between "science" and "religion," and biblical religion is having a hard time articulating its own faith in an age of science.

There are a lot of hidden confusions here, and it will take some work to sort them out.

Perhaps the basic idea that lies behind all this is the notion that if God is to act in the world, he has to push things around, just like I do when I step on the gas in my car or turn the steering wheel. Thus God takes his place alongside other actors in the world, and becomes one more like all the rest, even if his "pushing" is of a slightly different kind. Maybe his pushing on things can't be inspected the way the law of gravity can be, but it still has to be a "pushing" of some sort.

Thus an action not only has to have an intention, it also has to take effect in the real world by means of physical causes. This is the second assumption behind our dilemma.

This is where the collision with science happens. For science understands the notion of a physical cause in ways that make it very difficult to make sense of divine actions.

It is as if for God to act in the world, something in the world has to move over to make room for God to act. There has to be a hole cut in the world to make space for God to act. For God to act, he has to push on something, and for that to happen, ordinary forces have to stop pushing on that something, or he has to add his own force on top of whatever natural forces are also pushing on the thing that he has to move in order to act. Over and over again we will see this simple assumption, that the world has to make room for God to act, or else God can't act at all. It is a natural mistake, but a mistake nonetheless. It assumes that for God to act he has to come "into" the world and act the same way that other actors act in the world.

Even human actions are hard to make sense of from the point of view of physics. The foot moves, the car goes, the wheel turns, and the car turns, but all that is just physical motions, forces and levers. It is not a human action, it is just the motions of the body-parts in a human action. (You can call the body-parts the "material substrate," because that's what the person is composed of, but the person is more than just his material substrate, fond of it as he may nevertheless be.) We describe human actions in another language, a language of intentions, not the language of forces and motions. The language of physics is mathematics, but the language of action is narrative.

Nevertheless, in human actions as we commonly think of them, there is a material substrate, and the substrate moves. Physics can understand the material substrate and its motions even if it cannot understand or talk about the action itself. If divine actions are like human actions, they should work the same way.

Some questions arise at this point. Is such a "pushing" on the world a supernatural phenomenon? And if it were, what would "supernatural" mean? Does the language of action, divine or human, really work the way it appears to here?

To spill the beans, I don't think so. The concept of action and the language we use to speak of actions do not work the way our original dilemma assumes they do. Action is a concept from history, not from physics, and once the differences between thinking in historical terms and thinking in physical terms are seen, all these problems will go away. The rest of the book is an exploration of this sort of thinking. We begin with the problem in its original form, when people looked for God in physics, and show that even in terms of physics, it doesn't really make sense. Then, turning to history, things will begin to clear up.

Most of the book will be spent on history because thinking in history is still strange and unintuitive. It is not enough just to say that God doesn't make sense as a scientific explanation. After that, you have to see how thinking about a God of history works, or else the idea of God will come back seeking refuge in nature and the sciences.

1.2   Cause Laundering

If the problem for Christianity seems to come from science, some theologians have tried to defend religion in an age of science with ideas taken from recent physics. It is well known that at microscopic scales, the motion of sub-atomic particles is not deterministic. For these theologians, indeterminism opens up a realm of causation where God can act, giving God the tip of a long lever by which he could influence the motion of bodies at macroscopic scales. Physical causes are presumably traceable from the macroscopic domain to some microscopic scale after which they cannot be traced any further, and there God can act. When divine action has been conceived as "just like human action," and a very particular model of human action at that, this is the most natural way to ask whether divine action "really" happens in the world. In the end, I would prefer other ways to understand both divine and human action, and another sense of "really," but this one is close to the heart instincts of contemporary culture. Any discussion of acts of God today must at least implicitly take notice of it. Before looking for other ways to explain what is going on in acts of God, let's see how this one works.

What, then, is an "act of God," as it has appeared to those who want to find the acts of God in the microscopic interstices of physics? The tacit assumption is that acts of God make sense only if there are realms of physics where the behavior of bodies is not determined by physical law: then and only then is there room for objective acts of God. (This is how to cut a hole in the web of physical causation to make room for God to act.) Attributions of an event to an act of God and to deterministic explanation by physical law are taken to be mutually exclusive. The motions of physical bodies in regions where there are no physical causes can be ascribed to God. Presumably there is enough leeway so that God can influence the course of events and act in providential ways. (I have never seen actual calculations to show that there is enough leeway for God to act, but let that pass. It may not be a hard problem.)

One early example of this approach was William G. Pollard's *Chance and Providence* (1958), in which he argued that quantum uncertainty supplies just the indeterminacy that is needed to give God room to act. Pollard was a good physicist and a good theologian, but when he was doing philosophy of religion, he tended to switch back and forth from reasoning in physics to reasoning in theology without realizing what he was doing. Since then, many others have tried his same strategy, often more carefully, but not with any better results. I am dubious about whether the strategy itself will do what is demanded of it.

Usually, people assume that with quantum mechanics, the gaps in physical causation are essential and permanent and cannot be removed by any advances in knowledge of physics. If the gaps are irremovable, and if their indeterminacy allows enough room for God to act effectively, then they presumably would provide theology with breathing room and a secure realm that science cannot penetrate. It is this strategy and its tacit assumptions that I would like to contest, and I shall do it by stages. It is an assumption about the way to articulate biblical religion today, in the context of a scientific culture. At the beginning, it will be enough to see what is going on in the theological arguments about physics.

Opponents have called this approach "the God of the gaps," a derisive dismissal of it on the grounds that the gaps are not large enough to make a difference, or are evanescent and will evaporate with the course of progress in science. The phrase "God of the gaps" expresses the pathetic straits to which attempts to exhibit God within the language of physics had been reduced. But there is a deeper and more instinctive rejection of attempts to introduce God into nature in this way, because it is an intrusion into the integrity of nature. The grounds for rejecting providence by intrusions are at least as strong from the point of view of history as from that of physics, and we shall come to that in later chapters.

The "God of the gaps" was to act in regions of physics that we don't know *now*, gaps in present knowledge of how nature works. Theologians rejected such a strategy because those gaps in physical theory get filled with time and the progress of science. Any theological claims located in those gaps would be cut down like fresh grass before the lawn-mower of advancing scientific research.

The accusation of peddling a "God of the gaps" has been hurled at theologians by "atheists" for some time. But so far as I am aware, the notion of a "God of the gaps" was used first not by atheists but by a theologian. After reading in Weizsäcker's book, *The World-View of Physics*, Dietrich Bonhoeffer in a letter to Eberhard Bethge remarked on "how wrong it is to use God as a stop-gap for the incompleteness of our knowledge. . . . We are to find God in what we know, not in what we don't know. God wants us to realize his presence, not in unsolved problems but in those that are solved" (Bonhoeffer, 1971, p. 311). We are not to use God as a stop-gap for the incompleteness of what we know, but what is currently being proposed is not a stop-gap until future knowledge, but instead a program licensed by a permanent ignorance, one that is guaranteed ontologically. (How a program dependent on permanent ignorance (or even on what *cannot* be known) can be based on what we know rather than what we don't know baffles me.)

This way to make sense of divine action takes advantage of a simple feature of modern physics. For in physics, some things are *determined* by their causes, and other things, other motions, are random and *indeterminate*. This is true in many areas of physics, not just quantum mechanics, and in some places, the randomness is essential, where in other places it is just a convenient approximation for the physicist. It seemed impossible to make divine actions effective through determinate causes in physics, and so a refuge was sought in the indeterminate causes of physics.

If theologians are not careful, we shall be accused of cause laundering: In money laundering, drug lords put their money in bank accounts where it (or its sources) cannot be traced, and then it can be withdrawn and invested in "legitimate" businesses. Cause laundering is like money laundering. If causes can be traced to places where they cannot be traced any further, then a theologian is free to use them for his own purposes, such as ascribing them to "acts of God." Now classical chaos could be called classical cause laundering, because there are real causes that go into the laundry, and are untraceable when they come out. But quantum cause laundering is the drug lord's dream machine! There are *no* causes that go in, and yet effects come out, and they are guaranteed to be untraceable forever. If only drug money worked that way!

There are many problems with this approach. For only one, it is not clear what it would mean to say that physical causation can be traced back so far and no further—but agent causation *can* be traced back further than that limit. I think acts, especially divine acts, work differently from what has been tacitly assumed here, and we shall come to that soon enough. But first, there is more to be learned from examining the implications from physical theory for such a conception of divine acts.

1.3   The Hamiltonian of God

We can see how cause laundering works if we ask some questions. It would appear that if the alleged divine act makes a difference that is intelligible in terms of, in the language of, physics, it is "objective," but it is also a natural effect. If it doesn't make a difference intelligible in the language of physics, it's "subjective." What if alleged divine action makes a difference that is invisible, in quantum fluctuations? But if it changes the frequencies of random events, it's physics, and therefore a naturalistic effect. If it doesn't, it's subjective.

Consider what happens when you say that one event comes from God and another does not. How would you tell the difference? If the difference can be understood in terms of physics, if it is possible to exhibit a formula that tells when something comes from God and when it does not, then God and divine acts are reduced to a mere physical effect.

Suppose that we discover that we have one set of physical formulas to describe the motions of bodies under "natural" causes, and another set of formulas for the motions of bodies under "divine" causes. Yet we have physical equations for both kinds of motions. What is left of the claim that phenomena described by one set of formulas are to be ascribed to God, and those described by the other set of formulas are not? Why should *any* motions that are describable in physical terms be ascribed to God?

To put it another way, suppose that you can tell the difference between the motions of some physical body under the influence of divine action and the motions it would have had if there had been no divine action. If *this* question can be answered in physical terms, then we have in hand a physical formula for divine action. Scientists call this the "Hamiltonian." It is a complicated formula from which you can derive all the motions of a physical body. (You don't want to see one. They're sweet, but sometimes what you do with one is not, especially after you have customized it for a real-world problem.) Why, then is this Hamiltonian the Hamiltonian of God, and not just of another physical effect within the world?

Assume, then, that there is some way intelligible to physical theory that one can say the outcome, the physical motions, were different from what they would have been without an act of God. If you can do this, you can exhibit *within the terms of physical theory*, that is, in an equation, what difference God makes. If you can tell *in terms of physical theory* the difference between motions with and motions without divine action, then you might as well call it the Hamiltonian of God. Having identified that physical difference, you can also demarcate a physical phenomenon that can be identified with God. This is to draw God into the natural world on the natural world's own terms. All the alarms that should sound at this point are well warranted: for to locate God within nature on nature's terms is to compromise the transcendence of God, to turn Biblical religion into yet another variety of nature-worship. This is a very serious outcome indeed, for on its own terms, Biblical religion is then returned to the ancient nature cults out of which it emerged.

Look a little deeper. Why does physical determinism exclude divine action and physical indeterminism license it? What is the underlying assumption here? Why does any *natural* explanation, random as well as deterministic, rule out explanation as divine action? And does it really do so? Do the two kinds of explanation work the same way? Does one have to make room for the other? Are they mutually exclusive?

What sort of questioning is it that asks for a physical description of acts of God? What sort of questioning is it that asks for a physical concept of acts of God and then insists that such a physical concept be shielded from normal criticism? That it be physically invisible, undetectable? I would call it a theological *naturalism*, for it seeks to describe divine action in the same terms that in other parts of life are used to describe natural phenomena. But it is a very strange form of naturalism, for normally, when human beings construct naturalistic explanations, they are kept open to inspection and criticism by others. These explanations are not.

Theological naturalism assumes that in order to get God into the world, it is necessary to truncate something in the world to make room for God, to cut a hole in the world to make room for God. And so quantum indeterminacy would appear to be the ideal "hole" in the web of natural causation, because it is a hole that cannot be closed, a hole into which natural explanation cannot enter. It would then appear that divine action through quantum fluctuations is not really intervention into the natural web of causation. But if divine action cannot be identified in terms of physical theory, then it is not "objective" but instead "subjective," and subjectivity is what theological naturalism wants to avoid at all costs. If divine action can be identified in terms of physical theory, and if God is active in some events and not in all, then it seems to me inevitable that divine action really is an intervention into the natural web of causation.

The virtue of "objectivity" is purchased at the price of theological naturalism. "Objectivity" is a form of intellectual responsibility in the sciences. Eventually, a confessional approach, the sort of stance that was dismissed as "subjective," will turn out to embody the only kind of responsibility that one can have in religious matters. Most of this book will explore how that works. In religious commitments, to seek refuge in "objectivity" is a way to evade confessional responsibility. Before we come to the human element in religious commitment, let us look, in the next section, at how confessional commitments undergird the sciences, the realm of "objectivity."

1.4 Why Objectivity?!

Why the quest for objectivity in acts of God? What would they lack without it? And what is "objectivity," anyway? How did the dichotomy between "objectivity" and "subjectivity" arise? I put them in scare-quotes, because it is not entirely obvious what they are, or what they mean.

To say it a little differently, Why, if I can't describe them in terms of a physical formula, are acts of God then "only" in my mind? On the other hand, what is "subjectivity," and what is the problem with it? Why is it not enough?

This is quite a cluster of questions. It will take some unraveling. What I think lies at the bottom of this desire to explain acts of God in the terms of physical theory is a particular way of handling issues of responsibility. It will take some work to dig those issues out, so that they can be seen clearly.

We are a culture that trusts the natural sciences to deliver valid knowledge more reliably than any other human activity or mode of reasoning. The natural sciences enjoy a prestige that is unparalleled. In its more overt forms, this can be turned into a position that is articulated in a few simple claims: Natural science is the only way to get real knowledge, and science knows the world as it really is, exhaustively. There is nothing more to be known than what science knows. All other claims to knowledge are in fact not knowledge at all, but opinion, conjecture, superstition, wishful thinking, or worse. In former days, this position used to be known as "positivism"; today it is called "scientism."

In such a world, theology will have to pass itself off as "just like" the natural sciences, or else what it "knows" is not really knowledge. It has to use the same kind of thinking as the sciences, or forfeit all credibility. What it talks about has to be visible in the same way that physical effects are visible, or else it is not really there at all. It has to be "objective" and not "subjective," and acts of God have to be "objective" in the same way that physical effects are objective.

Yet on closer examination, science itself does not live up to the sort of "objectivity" that the myth of scientism ascribes to it. In order to get science going at all, it is necessary to make assumptions, and these assumptions can only be called "subjective" from the point of view of scientism. These assumptions command widespread assent today, but they were not at all obvious five hundred years ago. One of them is that the universe is orderly, that it is intelligible. It could be otherwise, as a few science fiction writers have realized, in their imagination of worlds in which magic works and is real. The orderliness of the universe is an assumption that is brought *to* the posing of problems that can be answered empirically, rather than derived *from* empirical results. It is not a result of any empirical test.

One can measure the *volume* of the universe, or its *mass*, or its *age*, but it makes no sense to try to "measure" its orderliness or its intelligibility. And this is what is necessary for an *empirical* claim: if you want to claim that you have determined in an experiment that the universe is "orderly," you have to devise an experiment, with several possible outcomes: some would show the universe to be orderly, some would show it to be disorderly. Age, mass, and volume are just a matter of measuring a number. Orderliness is a much richer concept, but it is also analogical in ways that age, mass, and volume are not. It is so elastic that it is very hard to pin down. "Order" has to be broad enough to encompass *all* the sciences, not just physics. The natural laws of chemistry and biology, while not contradicting those of physics, are also not reducible to them.

The failure to resolve any one scientific question is not evidence against the orderliness of the universe, but merely evidence that (perhaps) scientists were unimaginative or looking in the wrong place. Failure to resolve a scientific question now is no evidence that it will not be resolved in the future. And success in solving a scientific problem, in explaining one or another natural phenomenon, does not *prove* that any assumptions about the orderliness of the world are true. The assumption in question is about *all* the world, and success in explaining one phenomenon today does not guarantee success tomorrow in another. In every case of successful explanation in the sciences, the most that one could say is that the *assumption* of uniformity of laws of physics has *born fruit*. That does not prove it. And to say that it cannot be proven is not to question its truth, though evidently it appears that way to some people.

Why, then, do some need to believe that the orderliness of the universe is an empirical fact and not an assumption that makes possible empirical questions in the first place? Conceding that it is an assumption seems to be also an admission that it is subjective; the claim that it is empirical would also be a claim that it is objective. If the concept of "order," applied to the universe as a whole, *were* empirically testable, it would have to be expressible in the naturalistic language of one or another of the natural sciences. It is not. As noticed above, it is an analogical concept so elastic as to defy precise definition.

It is also a concept that presupposes the experience of human efforts to find order in particular naturalistic questions in the history of science. It is thus a concept that has a natural home in *historical* discourse. It is not a category of explanation *within* the language used to describe nature in the natural sciences, because it is *about* that language. It is nevertheless a way of describing nature, of saying something true about nature, but one that transcends the natural sciences. It must, because it is presupposed by those sciences.

Beneath the language of "objectivity" and "subjectivity" there is an issue of responsibility. If a claim is "objective," then I don't have to take responsibility for it, because it is in the equations, or in the empirical measurements. I can therefore responsibly demand assent to it from other people. If the claim is "subjective," then I am totally responsible for it, in the sense that it originates totally with me, but there is no way for such a claim even to challenge other people, much less make a responsible demand for assent from them. Outside of truly empirical questions, this is a very strange notion of responsibility: If I am responsible, I am incapable of responsibly asking agreement from other people! I think this description captures well the psychology of *misunderstanding* responsibility in cognitive claims, but it is not how things actually work. A better description of responsibility is possible, even for empirical claims.

In empirical claims, we expect a responsible scientist to explain his claims *about* nature in language that is naturalistic, i.e., just material and efficient causes, without invoking acts of God, magic, "miracles," or final causes. We expect his *scholarship* to be well informed about the history of previous scholarship in his field. We expect a scientist's claims to be expressed in a way that is open to testing by other investigators. And we know that when he uses uncontrolled or open-ended analogies, he is no longer making empirical claims, but is speaking as a theologian or a poet, even as a philosopher of science—but no longer as an empirical scientist.

Analogical claims can be held responsible, but questions of responsibility exhibit unique features when one asks about responsible use of analogy. It would beg the question to say that analogy can *never* be responsible. Clearly, some analogies do challenge, they do make claims on people, and when we acknowledge that an analogy is challenging, we usually credit those who use it with being responsible. Analogies are also notorious for being easy to wriggle out of: someone who doesn't like the claims of an analogy used against him is always free to say, "Those are your analogies," and walk away from them.

Analogies are always claims made by one person on others, they are always made in a community that has some shared experience. An analogy happens when we see one part of life in the light of another. Analogies accordingly have a human element that empirical and "objective" claims appear not to have. That human element is essential, it may not be forgotten or hidden without seriously misunderstanding what analogies mean or how they work. The key feature of responsibility is then not objectivity, but openness to other people's criticism. Human interpretations *can* be open to criticism.

Let me return to our example, the orderliness of the universe, and many people's anxieties lest the interpretive aspects of that claim expose it to a charge of subjectivity. When claims are made that are as broad and open-ended as the claim that the universe is orderly and intelligible, the most that a scientist can do is point to their fruitfulness, and *invite* others to accept them on the basis of that fruitfulness. That invitation will carry some real challenge, in the light of the history of science. But to misrepresent it as "objective" empirical proof is not to be responsible but to evade responsibility. The fruitfulness of a good analogy will show itself well enough, and in so doing, it will challenge other people quite sufficiently enough to qualify as responsible.

In effect, those who think the world ultimately has no order may be compared with those who trust that it is orderly. We see how both live, how both make sense of the cosmos. And each can be seen in the light of the other. In the end, you have to choose how you want to make sense of the universe.

The alert reader will have seen the parallels between the orderliness of the universe and (other) acts of God, for the logic of claims about both is very much the same. Analogies have been drawn in interpretation of the world, and some accept those analogies, but others simply walk away from them. We have stumbled into a practice of interpretation, and it needs to be explored before we go any further.

If we take the orderliness of the universe as an act of God, it is one that applies equally to all events, equally to all parts of the cosmos. The assumptions people bring to the question of cosmic order determine whether they can find such an order. Those assumptions are not empirical, and so are not "objective." Despite being "subjective," the reality they disclose is not unreal, and is not a figment of human imagination. But it is also a point of deep and apparently unresolvable disagreement, disagreements of the kind that happen between different basic life orientations. These disagreements are open to criticism, and they can be occasions of responsibility. Criticism of basic life orientations proceeds in a different way from criticism of theories *within* the sciences, which presupposes the orderliness of the universe.

We shall see that the same kind of logic applies when particular events are taken as acts of God. (This is called "Special Providence" in the technical language of theology.) The way to do that is to look at particular events, and since the alleged way that God acts is in physical events that are random, we should look at events that happen by chance. We shall also see, in the end, how disagreements about basic life orientation are handled responsibly.

Chapter 2

Other Possibilities

2.1   Lady Luck, Stern Fate

Look again at the idea that we can find acts of God in quantum fluctuations, impossible to penetrate in human knowledge, sometimes indeterminate, sometimes determined by divine forces that we cannot see. What is there to say that the agent in quantum fluctuations is really God, and not just Lady Luck or stern fate? In the ancient Hellenistic world, these were known as *Tyche* and *heimarmene*, and their cult attracted a large following.

The problem is not just that quantum fluctuations do not rescue us from the grasp of "subjectivism" (if it is that), but that they are open to multiple and radically different possible interpretations. Luck and fate really do not count as the same thing as the divine providence of Biblical religion. The difference is not merely that the analogies by which we speak of "actors" (luck, fate, God) are different. The import of events for human beings is different: if the unknown and uncontrollable future is a work of providence, then it brings blessing and life. If it is just luck, then it brings what is for the human recipients just chance. It may work out well, but good luck is not something to be grateful for. If it is fate, then it brings necessity, unchangeable, a kind of natural prison. We can ascribe an intention to events, and by analogy personify that intention as fate or luck. But then that intent is whimsy, capricious favor, vindictiveness, or manipulation. Or perhaps in the end, people are used as tools of some invisible and inscrutable purpose that cares nothing for us. In any case, it is not like the intentions of a benevolent parent who wishes what is best for the child, and it is this model of the benevolent father that is the center of the idea of divine providence.

There are abundant contemporary advocates of a basic life orientation that takes human life in the end to be a matter of fate or luck. And there are many who do so with a thoroughly scientific view of the world, working from the best science of our day. Jacques Monod will do as an example; his *Chance and Necessity* is a classic statement of the position. For chance is just luck, *Tyche*, and necessity is just fate, *heimarmene*. Recent popularizers of evolutionary theory such as Richard Dawkins, Daniel Dennett, and others like them have all argued in more or less the same way.

In the ancient world, Leucippus and Democritus are the outstanding examples. Their atomism presents a striking foretelling of modern atomic theory, in which the atoms have in themselves no macroscopic properties, are sub-microscopic, are not generated or destroyed, move in a void according to deterministic causes of blind necessity, rather than plan or purpose. Even the Atomists' cosmos resembles modern astrophysics in some ways. The ultimate desiderata are blind necessity; there is no chance.

There were advocates of a total scientific determinism in the eighteenth and nineteenth centuries. It is debatable today. Quantum mechanics in physics has made such a stand hard. The story of evolutionary biology has too many things in it that could scarcely be part of any deterministic plot that makes much sense. The impact of an asteroid causing the extinction of the dinosaurs is only the best known example. Events here are deterministic when taken one by one, but there is nothing coherent about them when they are taken all together. In that incoherence there is something like chance, and so the modern equivalent of *Tyche* appears again.

Today, one frequently hears evolution described in terms of "natural selection." This is an oxymoron: natural selection is like a square circle. In its original home, the word "selection" implies intelligence and purpose, but the adjective "natural" is intended precisely to deny intelligence and purpose. Biologists who speak of natural selection are quite candid in saying so. If we were to use strictly naturalistic language, then, we could speak only of random speciations and extinctions, and of the dynamics of genetic and ecological fluctuations leading to them. Whenever one hears the phrase "natural selection," one should be aware that something like the ancient Tyche and heimarmene is being invoked. More than just science is happening here. But it is important to emphasize for present purposes that it is a legitimate analogy—one *can* speak of fate or fortune (or "natural selection") in the light of physically indeterminate events. When the indeterminacy is "real" and not just lack of information, this language is both a practical analogy and also, more fundamentally, a basic way of looking at the world and human life in it. And if the indeterminacy is ontological, then there is no more basis that I am aware of for attributing the outcome of fluctuations to the God of historical-covenantal religion than to any of the naturalistic objects of human loyalty, such as Tyche, heimarmene, Democritus's atomism, or modern evolutionary natural selection. Or any less basis; it is a matter of interpretation.

I don't want to criticize such positions right now. It is enough to note that they are possible, and that they cannot be ruled out on the ground that science-and-religion harmonizers have set for themselves. For if the indeterminacy in nature is ontological, and truly indeterminate in an irreducible way, then it can be interpreted as the face of *Tyche* and *heimarmene* and their modern revivals just as easily as it can be taken as coming from acts of the God of biblical religion.

2.2   Turkey Day

Physical indeterminacy of events can be interpreted in quite different ways, and fate and fortune are only two. Look at a third, in which one gives thanks for some particular events. It is not just that this is the interpretation that I am interested in. It will show what is happening when people make sense of events. For there is an enormous liberty of interpretation here. Interpretation of events, of what they mean to the people involved, is restricted by the physical particulars of the events, but it is in no sense completely determined by those physical particulars.

The clue is in the words one hears from time to time about the annual American festival of Thanksgiving, at which a meal of roast turkey is traditional. The festival gets called just "Turkey Day." This should hint that something has changed, and more than just names, in the way this holiday is understood. When Thanksgiving is called "Turkey Day," there is no real thanks, or else real thanks are not permitted—reality leaves no room for the kind of thanks that were formerly offered at Thanksgiving.

Consider an example of a thank-worthy event, one from my own life. It is not so emotionally loaded nor so dramatic that it cannot be talked about without putting undue burdens on the reader, yet it was a significant turning point for me. In my senior year in high-school, we were asked to read R. G. Collingwood's *The Idea of History*. (We were also asked to read *The City of God*, which we found simply baffling.) Indeed, Collingwood was not easy, but I understood enough so that I could come back to it later, and then it assumed life-changing proportions, for it made clear how important it is for philosophers to look at history. I was grateful both to my teacher, Jim Vendettuoli, and to God, and said so, to both. (A good many years later, I detoured from visiting family and friends in Michigan to see Mr. Vendettuoli, as we called him when schoolboys. I think he was surprised; he was certainly delighted to be thanked.)

In the subsequent events as my life has played out in philosophy and theology, reading Collingwood early was indeed pivotal. When it came time to read German philosophers of history, Collingwood was already there as guide, and indeed, if it had not been for Collingwood, I might not have read them at all. Nor would I have made much sense of Mircea Eliade, who noticed the importance of history for certain kinds of religion.

One gives thanks to God for such a turn of events. But to *substitute* divine causation for human causation at this point would be a disservice and a disrespect to both God and to the humans involved. We have multiple ways of explaining the events: can they be located in multiple narratives? Or is it that they have multiple narrative connections? On one level, it was just a course in my senior year in high-school, albeit one that made a difference to me then, and a great difference later on. On another level, the level of my own development, a narrative in which sources of life and blessing are thematic, one can speak of acts of God, of providence.

Gratitude is the pivotal response, and gratitude extends beyond merely being grateful to the humans involved. They did not entirely know what they were doing, because what they were doing became what it was—the beginning of something—only later, when that "something" came to pass. What to do when your gratitude extends beyond the humans you are grateful to? Or when you are grateful, and the events came from natural and not human causes?

Indeed, what to do when you are not grateful? Or when you will not permit yourself an ontology that allows you something to be grateful *to*? When reality, as you understand it, doesn't leave room for anything to be grateful to beyond the ordinary actors within the world? When that's all there is? If you don't want to be grateful, such an ontology is a convenient way to avoid the problem. If you *do* want to be grateful, the problem is hopeless without language to handle it. If you do allow yourself something or someone to be grateful to in addition to ordinary actors, then there are multiple ways to speak of events, each with its own standards of meaning and responsibility, and each valid in its own realm.

One may even have humanly meaningful motives for rejecting gratitude: in some ways of looking at the world, gratitude is a vice, not a virtue. Robert Heinlein's *Stranger in a Strange Land* is fiction and neither philosophy nor history, but it makes the point eloquently. Jubal Harshaw, the grand old man of the story and informal instructor in how to live sums it up: "'Gratitude' is a euphemism for resentment." (Heinlein, 1987, p. 105). That's about as plain as it can be: for Jubal Harshaw (who is Heinlein's mouthpiece in the story), gratitude is a vice and not a virtue, and what it really means is resentment. (The connection to resentment is very real, but to go into that would take us way too far afield.) What is more, the *object* of gratitude, even on a merely human scale, is unreal. How much more so for divine acts?

It is clear that different attitudes are possible toward events. What does the believer do, when he looks at things ahead of time not knowing how they will turn out, and different outcomes are possible? In a situation of personal crisis, for the Christian believer (and I don't think Jews are any different, the Talmud is clearer than the New Testament) *any* possible outcome will be regarded as providential. Whatever happens, the believer will treat it as an indication of how to proceed. As a *divine* indication of how to proceed. It is the raw material with which to continue life. The biblical believer is grateful, at least in principle. And that gratitude anticipates a larger story in which the good of events will be made actual, when the reasons for being grateful are clear instead of just a matter of trust. This is so even if the immediate sorrow of events is overwhelming.

So we have some serious problems with the naive model of God choosing one outcome and bringing it about through physical *causes* that we could conceive or understand. And the naturalistic model for divine action assumes that God's actions have causal connections that could be traced back to God, in the same way that we trace physical causes. For the believer, when events could turn out in two ways, either way is received as providential. Only one will be met with simple rejoicing—the one that was desired. But the other will not be rejected as barren; it will be reappropriated as a blessing that is not yet patent, or as a challenge to work on. This should open the way to questions not just about how *events* are characterized, but also about how human *actions* are to be characterized, since it is in human actions that we make clear how we receive and interpret events. For we make clear what goods we seek in events by the actions we take in response to events. And it is by analogy with human actions that we speak of divine actions.

At this point, we have uncovered some real problems with the notion that for there to be an action, there have to be both an intention and a physical pushing on something to make the intention actually happen. This assumption was at the root of our original dilemma, the conflict between science and religion. We shall see that there are more problems still with this underlying assumption.

2.3   Cruising

Visualize, if you will, a seventeen-year old male driving down the main street of a modest-sized town in a polished 1956 Chevy. Ask yourself, what is he doing?

Is he going to the store to get dogfood and milk?

Trying to avoid household chores?

Bored with TV?

Seeking relief from summer heat in a house with no air conditioning?

Trying to recharge the car's battery?

Fleeing from a family quarrel at home?

If I tell you that he is only going four miles per hour, it is 8:30 on a Friday evening in August, and all the other traffic, pedestrian as well as vehicular, is of comparable age, then I think it becomes clear exactly what he is doing.

This is not a question that any naturalistic definition can answer. For any naturalistic definition of cruising can be altered or defeated by simply changing the circumstances in other parts of the lives of the people involved. When the City Council of Livermore (where I live) passed an ordinance against cruising, they merely indicated the offense as "passing the same intersection more than three times in an hour", or some such contrived definition. The law can be looser than philosophers. (I have a friend who once upon a time had to go to the store four times in the course of baking one cake, and she most certainly was not cruising.)

It will not do to postulate some criterion based on "what's happening in the brain of the kid in the car." He may have been thinking about his trigonometry homework (how do you set up spherical coordinates in four dimensions in two qualitatively different ways?). And cruising nonetheless. Or not cruising at all, really just doing trig in a traffic jam. And suppose there is a mature adult driver among these cars—is the adult just in a traffic jam, or is the adult also cruising?

Or our teen-age driver may have been trying to figure out how to read Proverbs 7 with a straight face in church the next Sunday morning. (Pastor may not have been thinking when he assigned the lesson.) And she may or may not be cruising, if I may change our protagonist to a girl of late teen years. To know, one would have to know her, and know enough about the rest of her life to tell whether cruising is the sort of thing she would do.

To put it simply, for any naturalistic *definition* of what cruising is, I can invent a *story* in which the physical motions of the protagonist meet the definition, and yet the particulars of his life "off-stage," beyond the limits of what the definition looks at, make it quite clear that he is not cruising at all. It is cheating, by the way, to try to pass off as naturalistic a claim that "intent to cruise" can be identified by naturalistic means, or could, in principle, if we could just get a "memory dump" of what's in the kid's brain. Intent to cruise, or to do any other thing, is a matter of how the physical motions of an act are to be fitted into larger narratives. And narratives can be told in many ways. Told *truthfully* in many ways. If the memory dump merely selects one of those narratives, then we don't have a naturalistic definition of the act we are looking for, we have merely asked our teen-age driver what he is doing. Calling a definition naturalistic doesn't make it so.

A traffic jam is quite different from cruising, even though their physical motions are virtually the same: a lot of cars crowded into one street and not going very fast. A naturalistic or scientific description really can't say much beyond what the physical motions are. The language of human action is about something more than just the physical motions. It uses terms that combine a sense of what the motions are, some indication of the larger narrative that they fit into, the purpose or intent of the actions, and some idea of the probable consequences for the actors.

A naturalistic account of events is presumably unique; once one has identified the physical motions and their physical causes, there are no alternative naturalistic accounts of the events. Certainly this is true in physics; equations of motion generally have unique solutions. But *all* of the above accounts of the human actions may be simultaneously true. This kid may have been going to the store, recharging the battery, avoiding circumstances at home, doing trig homework, and even savoring Proverbs 7. In addition to cruising. Which narrative fits best is a matter of the larger circumstances in the lives of all the people concerned.

We can see that questions about human action are very different from questions about physical motion or physical causation. Indeed, there are two kinds of language here, and concepts such as "act," "intent," and so on have meaning only in one kind of language, and (physical) "cause" has meaning only in the other. The fact that historians also speak of "causes" in history only confuses matters, for causation in history does not work in entirely the same way as it does in physics. There *are* physical motions in human actions, or at least in some human actions, but they are usually not described in the terms of physical causation. And there are human actions, actions for which we hold people responsible, where the motions are negligible or completely absent. Acts of omission and acts of consent, for example. We can frequently relate the language of human experience and human action to the language of the natural sciences, but we do not do so by translating one into the other. We do not reduce one to the other. There is no "isomorphism" between them, as a mathematician would say. Instead, we come to something like a diagnostic appraisal, much as a doctor figures out what is happening physically from what the patient experiences.

Some people would like to claim that naturalistic language is the only language that can deliver "real" truth. Naturalism claims that its language can describe any phenomenon, and so that its language is the only one necessary. Any other language makes sense, can speak truth, only insofar as it can be translated into naturalistic language. Now this is an interesting claim. For it says it can abstract from all human involvements and still speak truth. We have seen that such a claim has serious problems merely in our example of a kid going to the store to get bread and milk. Human action is about human concerns, and the language of human action tell us about those concerns. The language of divine action, modeled by analogy on the language of human action, will work the same way.

Chapter 3

Strangely Familiar Language

3.1 Tickets to Bali H'ai

Once upon a time there was a debate, a debate about the existence of God. On one side was a philosopher, Wallace Matson, against the so-called existence of God, and on the other side was Edward Hobbs, a theologian, arguing for God. Matson began. The audience was warmed up, full of excitement, and he was having a good time. As he wound up his peroration, he turned from Edward Hobbs to the audience and back again, and said, "Edward, you people have been selling tickets to Bali H'ai, only there ain't no such island!" It looked as if God was out of luck.

Hobbs got up and laughed and said, "Why yes, Wally, of course we have; but why did you take your ticket to the Embarcadero instead of to the Coronet Theater?"

Things apparently did not go very well for the atheists in what followed, and they attributed this to the superior rhetorical skills of professor Hobbs. But really, these few one-liners capture the essence of the misunderstanding about language of God, and also the misunderstanding about how divine action works.

Some examples can show us how the language of human action works. They are fictional, but fiction uses much the same techniques of narrative language that history does. We shall come to history in due course.

Consider The Far Side, the one-panel comic strip that ran for much of the 1980s. I particularly remember one scene, of a plump and dowdy old woman leaning over a waist-high boxy thing with some dials and knobs on it. Over the hill in the background is the head of a dinosaur looking at this scene. She does not yet see the dinosaur. The caption is, "Professor McCready's cleaning lady mistakes his time-machine for a clothes dryer."

Like most humor, The Far Side turns on an inversion, a surprise, something that was not expected going into the scene. We are treated to a view of someone unknowing, whose plans will be upset as the action moves to its inevitable conclusion. Often the players are animals who talk. Two spiders weave a web across a playground slide, saying to each other, "we'll eat like kings for years!", when of course the web won't even be seen by the kid who crashes through it coming down the slide. Cows in a pasture pretend to be dumb whenever a car comes, but otherwise hold a quite sophisticated conversation standing erect on their hind legs when no-one is watching.

Who is more fooled? The people, or the cows? We are revealed to be frail, knowing less than we think, and soon to be frustrated. There is a technical term for this; theologians call such beings "creatures," and creaturehood is precisely the state of being not-self-made, not-in-control, and so on. Now a lot of scientists particularly liked The Far Side, and perhaps they thought that just because it had a lot of dinosaurs in it, it was in favor of evolution, and so not "religious." These animals instruct the humans in what it means to be really human, to be not-in-control, and so on. How does one acknowledge that the Far Side is *true*? Not in philosophy, but by just laughing. Philosophy runs too much risk of denying the very truth that it pretends to acknowledge. It is quite sufficient merely to enjoy the cartoon.

Consider a longer example, and one that has some plot. Not quite *South Pacific*, but almost. Art may be fiction, but fiction wouldn't be interesting if it didn't tell us something about real life. *Mad Max (III): Beyond Thunderdome* probably appealed first to an audience's sense of adventure and the thrill of a post-nuclear-war survival story. This movie shares more than one might think with *South Pacific*. Rogers and Hammerstein can sing for us, "Dites-moi, pourquoi, la vie est belle," in a story that has sorrow and death enough, but is a romance for all its dangers. For it relies upon a larger world that is stable, a framework that is unambiguously positive. The children's song does not lie, it speaks fairly for the movie. *Thunderdome* assumes a larger background that is at best ambiguous. There is not much left after a nuclear war (one that we never see) but Australian desert and a few people struggling for a very marginal survival. Radioactive fallout is a fact of life. Food and fuel and water are scarce. Electricity is available only by contrivance. Yet electricity is the life-blood of what these people take to be really living, real culture, real blessing. The struggles to make it, to control it, and to control the people who make it dominate the life of the town where the movie begins. But what we see first are the totems of personal adornment. Of mass-produced clothing there is no more; rags and contrivances and wearable hardware have come to be badges of defiance, icons of survival, of power, of can-do, of adventure. Icons of a way of life.

The Mad Max of two previous movies is a survivor who used to have a real job in a real society before . . . before the Fall, one wants to say. He has been reduced to driving an old truck drawn by camels, because there is not fuel enough to run its engine. It looks like poverty, but it is wealth. Though he looks like a bag-lady, bag-ladies do not drive trucks, even trucks that have run out of gas. Our hero is thrown into a place called Bartertown. A father and son team spies him from their tiny aircraft, the Flying Jalopy, and they steal his truck and camel team, and take it into Bartertown to sell it. Bartertown is a spot of life in the desert, a lot of people trading, partying, quarreling, attempting to re-establish the fabric of civilization, the sense of a larger framework of stability in the cosmos. For the most part, they fail. What is civilized is mostly just relics, fragments, broken parts of machinery now turned into totems almost magical, since the machines and machine culture of which they were a part no longer work or no longer exist. Life is precarious and marginal in Bartertown, and party though they may, its inhabitants do not really celebrate. They struggle to survive.

One wonders whether the movie producers had anthropological consultants help them design the sets, the totems and clothing, the sense of magic in place of technology. Perhaps they just wanted colorful scenery and some good chase scenes. They had a good actor in Mel Gibson, one who could draw crowds, and they needed a plot for a sequel to the second movie in the series. Whatever they intended, whether they knew it or not, they made more than just another Mad Max movie.

The central icon of the town is a steel-frame dome over an open sand lot, with girders spaced at intervals that people can climb on easily. This is the "Thunderdome" of the movie's title. It is very much like a playground structure for children, but it is large enough, scaled up, so that really big kids (sometimes known as adults) can play on it. The crowd clambers up over the dome and looks down on two contestants in the center. It is a sort of amphitheater inverted, with the audience above the players, looking down from the roof.

Mad Max is not only thrown into Bartertown, but, as matters unfold, into a contest in the Thunderdome. Unlike children's games, this one is to the death. Dr. Dealgood, the Em-Cee, is garbed in the sort of black robe that preachers and judges used to wear when there was civilization. Such a robe suits him well as he warms up the crowd. His spiel rehearses Bartertown's cosmology, the harvest of war that destroyed civilization. Thunderdome contains human quarrels before they can become wars. Its hand-to-hand combat also provides entertainment for the whole town: a ritual drama that exhibits the cruel meaning of life: "Dyin' time's here."

The fight commences when Auntie Entity (played by Tina Turner) announces solemnly, "This is Thunderdome, and death's listening. He'll take the first man who screams." The narrator a little later speaks of a "pitiless post-holocaust world where any weakness marked a man as a victim." Such is the outlook of Bartertown; the cosmos is chaos, and it is against them. What happens in the Thunderdome is the central drama of the meaning of life.

As things turn out, Mad Max survives only to face what is a simultaneous parody of a TV game show and of the American legal system, the Wheel of Fortune. (Can the Australian legal system be as bad as the one in America?!) The wheel is spun, and following its instructions, Max is sent into the desert bound on a horse to die. The horse dies. He almost does.

Abandoned in the desert, unconscious from thirst, he is found by a tribe of children who live by an oasis stream at the bottom of a small canyon, far from Bartertown. They drag him to their habitat, nurse him back to consciousness. It happens that these children were passengers on a jetliner that crashed in the war; they think Mad Max is the pilot, Captain Walker, who left to get help, and promised to return. They have preserved their story in an oral tradition, carefully re-told, with much excitement, so that they might not be unprepared when help comes to save them. They have a *history*. Though Mad Max denies being Captain Walker, in the end, they do fly out for help, and they do so with Mad Max's help. On the way, these kids sneak into the bowels of Bartertown and steal the locomotive that was used to generate electricity. There is a grand chase scene, one with most of Bartertown screaming across the desert, a fleet of motor vehicles cobbled together from a chassis here, a motor there, mostly go-karts of a size for big boys to play in. They try to apprehend the kids, but the kids escape. In the final scenes, they get off airborne in the Flying Jalopy that had been used to steal Mad Max's truck and camel team at the start of the movie. Mad Max is left groaning in pain in a wreck as Aunty Entity stands over him smirking, and says to him, "You're just a raggedy man!" She spares him and the movie ends.

Even the movie reviewers detected parallels with Christ in this plot. But that is by no means the only external reference the movie carries, and it is not the most helpful one, because Christ-parallels have become like a gilded lily, once beautiful, but so over-decorated and falsely adored that the native beauty is utterly covered up.

There is another movie in which a group of young schoolboys are put on a jetliner escaping from nuclear war. The plane crashes, and they are marooned on an island not far from Australia. What follows is the unfolding of original sin in the very children who are often thought to be uncorrupted and sinless. These boys turn into savages rather quickly. The irony is emphasized when the worst of them are in the school choir, and they first appear marching down the beach, chanting the *Kyrie Eleison* (Lord, have mercy) as their fight-song. They are eventually rescued by adults who find them as the movie ends. But they are rescued only in the trivial sense that the adults return them to the "normal" world in which their savagery is covered up, and so the problem of the movie goes unsolved. In *Thunderdome*, by contrast, the kids, because of their faithfulness to a narrative tradition, are open to a different kind of rescue. Those who have seen *Lord of the Flies* can only groan in delight as *Thunderdome* unfolds.

Each movie is transformed when its horizon is expanded to include the others. Remember what we saw in the kid who was cruising on an August Friday night? The only way we could really know what he was doing was to know what was going on in his life beyond that summer evening. To know what is happening here and now, we have to know what is happening in larger and larger circles around the here and now. In the same way, each of our three movies changes the meaning of the other two.

3.2   Beyond Thunderdome

To see what is happening—in all three movies, not just *Thunderdome*— listen to the story the kids by the oasis tell themselves. Mad Max is lying unconscious, nearly dead of thirst, and the kids have hauled him down into the canyon oasis where they live. They have put him on a platform of boughs and reeds some distance above the pool of the creek. They think he is Captain Walker (we do not yet know who Captain Walker is), and they have taken the precaution of tying a cable of vines to one ankle, so that he can't get away.

With a lot of excitement, one of them, Savannah, points him out to another kid in with a mixture of awe, rejoicing, and triumph. They don't know what Captain Walker looks like, so there is some doubt, but she is sure it is he. Yet is this too good to be true? Their "word-stuff" is degenerate street slang, even more so than the language of Bartertown. They don't know how to talk to him, and think he is not so much unconscious as out of radio contact, so they try hailing him on a "radio" that is just a congeries of old parts that doesn't even have any electricity in it.

But Mad Max wakes up on his own, recovered some from thirst, thanks to the water they have poured into his mouth in his sleep. Startled, he falls off the platform and dangling like a jumper on a bungee-cord, he is dipped into the pool below. Thoroughly wet now, and wide awake, he can answer questions. They tell him they have been waiting for him, and he asks, "Who do you think I am?" (Viewers who know the Synoptic Gospels would have a hard time keeping a straight face at this point, but things do not entirely play out as they did between Jesus and his students.) They tell Mad Max they have kept everything straight, everything marked, everything remembered. He still doesn't know what's going on, he doesn't know who they think he is.

And they are just as perplexed that Mad Max doesn't understand. They are afraid that they have not been faithful to the instructions of Captain Walker, who left to get help and promised to return and rescue them. But they have been faithful, they have gone to great trouble to remember and be ready. Slake, one of the older boys (still a teenager, young by Bartertown standards), begins, and announces the ritual in the words, "Here's the Tell." One of the other kids takes a pole about the size of a broomstick with a square of small pruned boughs lashed to the end, a square about the size of a TV screen, and holds the square up to successive pictures chalked up on the wall of the canyon.

Max knows the "real" history, the history as it is told in Bartertown, and it is a story of disaster, the aftermath of a nuclear war, the end of "civilization as we know it," and a time of deprivation and death. Life is scarce. He begins to realize how the kids in the Tribe tell their story to themselves, and he plays along, trying to figure out what game he is playing with them. He begins to catch on to who they think he is.

Slake begins, but he passes the story to Savannah, and she continues. It is the story of the whole Tribe, and they have treasured it so they can pass it on. Lifespans are short, mothers give birth in their teens, and so the time from one generation to the next is not long.

The story begins with how they got where they are, with the "pox-iclips," the nuclear war, and their flight on a jetliner to escape it. The jet crashed, in the Australian desert. Captain Walker went to get help and left instructions that they should stay and wait, but also that they should tell the youngest what they were doing, and why. In the time of disaster, in their slang, Mister Dead caught many, but he couldn't catch Walker. The plane crashed, some of them lived, and they came here to the creek oasis in the desert. They have a hand-held slide viewer and a few picture slides of life before the change, their only real memories of civilization. And a few slides without much context picture a culture that is transformed in the light of memory into something almost magical. The story continues. When Walker left, his parting words were, "Wait! one of us will come!" And so the kids protest that they have kept all their hopes and memories together, that they have waited as instructed. They are afraid that if they have disobeyed, Captain Walker will not rescue them.

Mad Max begins to realize what has happened. He plays along with them, but also wants to be realistic. The interchange continues. The kids think their dreams are coming true, he really is Captain Walker. He is going to take them to Tomorrow-morrow Land! But he protests, explains that he is not Captain Walker.

The kids take Mad Max out to the wreck of the plane they came on, evidently a very large commercial airliner, now half-covered with sand, all its paint sand-blasted off in the desert wind, leaving only etched gray aluminum of the plane's giant tail-fin. Kids climb up onto the back of the fuselage, and some shinny up all the way to the top of the tail-fin.

Later, at the end of the movie, after they have indeed been rescued and flown out of the canyon oasis, when some of them are a good deal older, they remember, they still remember, but the prologue of The Tell has been changed slightly. It begins with a reminder to remember, to pass the story on, because the story belongs to everybody, and in the long haul, with its uncertainties, hazards, and mishaps, this is the story that holds people together, shapes life, and gives life. Their story is remarkably biblical—these are the generations of Abraham, this is how we came into the Promised Land, this is how our forefathers, etc. It would do passably as a theology of the Fall into original sin and redemption from sin, very Augustinian, very Christian. Or it could be read like the second half of the Shema: "Take these words to heart which I enjoin on you today. Drill them into your children. Speak of them at home and abroad, whether you are busy or at rest." We shall have a slightly different version of our Tell in a few pages, but Thunderdome is a good place to start.

South Pacific is a romance, and one beloved for its story. But if World War II had turned out differently, life would have gone on, differently, but not in chaos. The world was safe, even if few of the characters in the movie were entirely safe. In *Lord of the Flies* and in *Thunderdome*, the world is not safe. Chaos threatens to overwhelm Mad Max's world, and William Golding's world in *Lord of the Flies* shows us a more horrible reality within the boys who play on its screen.

South Pacific legitimately sets aside the problem of the other two movies, in order to give us the romance that won the hearts of a generation of Americans who fought in the Pacific War. *Lord of the Flies* and *Thunderdome* confront the problem. It has a technical name among theologians, "original sin." This term does NOT meant original guilt, but instead a propensity to be discontented, to reject one's status as a creature, the sort of being who is subject to unattractive limitations, who doesn't really know (or who even conceals) what is going on, even in his own life, who is surrounded by neighbors whose needs jeopardize his own survival.

Some contrasts: Bartertown has no history, or at least not one that you would like. For them, history is barren. The world of *Lord of the Flies* has lost its history. *South Pacific* assumes its larger history, one in which World War II challenges order but never threatens to abolish it utterly, to undermine it as if it had never been. The human predicament has been tamed, it is not a fundamental threat. But the means by which it came to be not-a-threat have been hidden and at once forgotten and taken for granted.

Look at how the Tribe in *Thunderdome* lives, for they are the key to all three movies. History does not exempt the Tribe from the world it shares with Bartertown, but it does give them a sure and certain hope. They are a people in travel, on the way, moving through a history that has a promise, one they cannot see but only trust will come. Where the cosmos for Bartertown was ultimately chaos and hostile to boot, the cosmos for the Tribe is a promise, and is on their side. Where in *South Pacific*, the universe is on the side of the good guys, its order is never fundamentally threatened. In *Lord of the Flies*, we see the human predicament in need of help from outside, with only stark prospects absent that help. (If I may be permitted a wink to theologians, *Lord of the Flies* is the most Barthian of the three movies.)

The culture of Bartertown is shared by the Tribe. Totems of magic and personal power are the rule in one as in the other. There is not less poverty in the Tribe than in Bartertown, but more. Bartertown is wealthy by comparison, and has no hope. The Tribe's hope is something that you could call "subjective," if you were not in the mood to share it. And what they hope for is a kind of outside help, and that is where we began this book. For there is a technical term for "outside help"; insurance brokers and theologians alike call it "acts of God."

The boys in *Lord of the Flies* need help but cannot imagine or conceive it. *South Pacific* doesn't really need it, for its world is safe. Bartertown wants none. The Tribe has a history, and their *past* history makes sense only with their *future* history. This movie, fiction though it be, makes a claim on us, and if we side with the Tribe, we acknowledge that claim as *true*.

So-called "acts of God" can be viewed from many perspectives, and fiction is only one of them. There are others.

3.3   TV Ads

You are listening to the radio in the car. There are two voices:

First voice: "Are you sure we should be up here at this time of night, looking in someone's bedroom window like this?"

Second voice: "Oh, yes, I do this with prospective customers all the time. Think nothing of it; this is normal."

First voice: "Sure looks quiet in there; they must be really sound asleep."

Second voice: "Would you like to go in? Get a closer look?"

First voice, in shock and horror: "Oh no! I wouldn't go into someone else's house in the middle of the night without permission!"

Second voice: "Oh, don't worry; they're used to it." He slides the window up, with a little noise, and we hear some very gentle snoring. They clamber in. The snoring continues undisturbed.

The salesman gently nudges one of the sleepers, and says, "Mrs. Hogan, I'd like to introduce Mr. Smith, he'd like to see how your mattress feels."

With some effort, she wakes, and in the happy voice of sweet dreams, welcomes the salesman, and gets out of bed. She invites Mr. Smith, the prospective but still hesitant customer, to lie down in the bed to see how it feels. He protests that her husband is asleep in the bed! She assures him that her hubby is used to it, turns to her husband, and says, "Wake up, dear, we've got company!"

He protests at getting into bed with a strange man, but she will have none of it, and departs to make tea for her guests. He lies down in the bed and is immediately relaxed—and amazed—by its softness and comfort. Then we hear the pitch—for a mattress company, and a telephone number to call for the nearest dealer.

Preposterous? Of course. All advertisements are. We would be disappointed if they were not. In a TV advertisement, we are treated to entertaining and hyperbolic claims for the product, and then invited to purchase. We know there is a product, and we know that we are being invited to purchase it. Without the hyperbolic and preposterous (and often unphysical!) claims, we could never get so easy a sense of what the product can do for our lives.

Now remember a few advertisements that you are somewhat more familiar with.

"Suppose one of you has a friend and goes to him in the middle of the night to say, 'My friend, lend me three loaves, because a friend of mine on his travels has just arrived at my house and I have nothing to offer him'; and the man answers from inside the house, 'Do not bother me. The door is bolted now, and my children and I are in bed; I cannot get up to give it you'. I tell you, if the man does not get up and give it to him for friendship's sake, persistence will be enough to make him get up and give his friend all he wants."

From almost the same source, "The kingdom of heaven is like treasure hidden in a field which someone has found; he hides it again, goes off happy, sells everything he owns and buys the field."

In another, a gospel preacher was warming up the crowd in the house where he was preaching. Some men with a paralytic friend couldn't get in, so they climbed up on the roof, and dug a hole in the roof, and lower their friend down through the hole on a body-bag. The preacher said to the man, "My child, your sins are forgiven." After some friction with his crowd, who do not entirely believe that sins *can* be forgiven, he says to the paralytic, "I order you: get up, pick up your bag, and go off home." This story is noticeably more preposterous, noticeably more like TV ads.

But what is the product? And would you buy it?

Does the Bible really use the same sort of language as TV ads do, to make a point about real history? Why *shouldn't* the Bible use the same repertoire of literary techniques as we are used to in everyday life? (For those who want a superb technical exposition of this claim, it can be found in an article by Edward Hobbs from 1974). Some of my students eventually caught on to me and took fright; they complained that sacred texts should not be read this way.

But does "sacredness" here defend against the real message?

In the end, the question of the comics and TV ads and the Bible alike (and they are alike) cannot be evaded: are they *true*? And what "are they *true*" really means is, Is the product any good? Is this how life really is? Is this where it's at? I once thought that this question could not be evaded by switching into a naturalistic kind of language, the language that takes the texts "literally" (whatever that might mean), and then goes on to invoke naturalistic means for acts of God. Oh, but it can! It can! Evading the challenge of the texts is *exactly* what a naturalistic interpretation does!

Chapter 4

Theology Bewitched

4.1   By the Waters of Naturalism

> By the waters of naturalism we sat down and wept,
>> when we remembered you, O land of History.
>
> As for our guitars, we hung them up
>> on the trees in the midst of that land.
>
> For those who led us away captive asked us for a song,
> and our oppressors called for mirth:
>> Sing us one of the songs of History.
>
> How shall we sing for the Lord of History
>> on an alien soil?
>
> If I forget you, O land of History,
>> let my right hand forget its skill.
>
> Let my tongue cleave to the roof of my mouth
> if I do not remember you,
>> if I do not set life in History above my highest joy.

Permit me this parody of Psalm 137. It is a metaphor of historical religion captive on the alien soil of naturalism.

Psalm 137 is a psalm of the Exile, when little Judah was hauled off to Babylon captive in 586 BCE, after Nebuchadnezzar sacked and burned Jerusalem, and permanently ended the kingdom of Judah and with it the House of David. (This is *the* Babylonian Captivity.) The psalm comes from the experience of being taunted for the entertainment of her captors. Taken captive, transported to an alien land and treated as beneath contempt, slaves or little better, mocked, it is easy to empathize with the bitterness we hear in this Psalm.

Religion in the modern world (or at least the religion of Christianity and Judaism in the modern world) faces a predicament uncomfortably like this. We live in a culture where anyone can claim that science has disproven religion, science has replaced religion, and whether or not he is *believed*, he will be *understood*. Christianity used to shape European culture, and theology was the queen of the sciences. Today, Christianity has lost much of its credibility. Theology is a bag-lady. Nowhere is biblical religion well explained enough to have an immediate and intuitive plausibility. Only those brought up in it well enough to know how to work its arcane language can use it to make sense of their lives. It is not that America lacks believers; it is far more religious than Europe. But Christianity has lost enough of its ability to explain itself so that its enemies (and there are some) can now attack it more or less openly.

I contend that much of the problem (and the only part of it that we look at in this book) comes from confusions about nature and history, especially about how a historical religion works. These pains began in the 1600s. The new science of Galileo, Newton and Boyle, and the philosophy of Descartes and Locke and their successors in the eighteenth century, all worked to put the world in a new light. (A hundred years after them, history also came to be seen in a new light, and two hundred years after them, history was beginning to be understood in ways it never had been before, but that is to get well ahead of our story.) The new science and the new philosophy were worked out by people who were all devout Christians or Jews, and so it looked like things would all turn out "for the greater glory of God."

Things did not work that way. Soon, the new science looked like it would explain everything, leaving nothing for God to do. God was unemployed.

Now there is at least one difference between the Babylonian Exile and the modern-day conflicts between science and religion. The Babylonians were foreigners, and Judah was conquered by a hostile power. But modern science was a child of religion, it was as if the child had turned against the parent. (It was only because the scientists believed in an all-powerful God who could impose laws on nature that they thought they could understand nature, and so do science at all.) So despite the dissimilarities between the Exile and modern science and religion, there is some of the same feeling of Psalm 137 in the latter-day difficulties of religion in a world of science. Perplexity might be better than bitterness, for religion today has trouble understanding itself, and even more trouble explaining itself in a world of science.

A little history may help. The physicists (Robert Boyle prime among them) sought to make sense of acts of God in terms of the new physics that they had invented. This was to be an act of praise, an offering of first-fruits to the God who had made their work possible. Things did not work that way. For the English physicists imagined acts of God to have efficient causes in the new way that the motion of bodies was understood in physics. Philosophers in France (and later, Hume, in England) demolished this idea like a house of cards. Many of the faithful, however, had bought into the crucial assumption, and naturalistic theology was born at this time. (For those who want the details, R. M. Burns's book (1981) gives a very readable account.) In naturalistic theology, acts of God have to be understandable in the terms and in the language of modern science.

Some definitions are in order. Formerly (and still, among those who care), God was thought to be transcendent to the world. Now transcendence is a concept easily misunderstood, and even the word is not more than a few centuries old. In the simplest sense, transcendence just means going beyond, something outside. But if one thing (God) is outside of another (the world), what is to stop us from just expanding the world to include God, and now God is no longer really outside the (enlarged) world? It doesn't help much to say, "Don't talk that way," because people always *can* talk that way, and so the meaning of the idea of God is permanently changed. Changed for the worse.

The word "immanence" used to mean the presence of the transcendent within the world, and if you do it right, transcendence *always* includes an immanent presence. It is not something stuck outside trying to get in, locked out by natural laws that won't let it in, like a kid peeking through the window unable to attract attention from the people inside. What is "immanent" is completely different from the "intramundane." What is "immanent" is always the presence of something transcendent. The "intramundane" means what it says in Latin—what is inside the world, but it means what is *just* inside the world, part of the world and of the workings of the world, explicable in the terms of the world without any reference to anything transcendent.

Now we can see how the modern sciences got started. For they decided they were not interested in purposes, human or otherwise (Aristotle called these "final" causes). Instead, they would look only at what they called "material causes" and "efficient causes." To ask about material causes is just to ask what something is made of. (Chemistry tells a lot about material causes.) Efficient causes were the realm of the new physics, because an efficient cause is the kick by one thing that makes another thing move. And motion is the real interest of physics. More grandly, the sciences are a search for intelligible intramundane connections between intramundane phenomena. (Actually, the sciences are interested in only a certain very limited kind of intramundane connections.) We just want to know "how things work," in intramundane terms. Since God is about transcendence, God is ruled out as an explanation in the sciences. To do science at all, you have to assume that there *are* intelligible intramundane connections between intramundane phenomena. *This* assumption requires some knowledge of transcendence, for it is not something that those intramundane connections could explain. They display it, but they do not explain it. To assume that the natural world is intelligible is an act of faith, the faith that the world is orderly. There are people enough who do not believe that, though they have a bad reputation these days. This act of faith came from latter-day biblical religion, for it was the God of biblical religion who made the world orderly and intelligible. And so it was the better instincts of religion itself that insisted that God is not to be an explanation in the natural sciences.

This world-view is a lot different from what we call *philosophical* naturalism, the idea that nature is all there is, and there is nothing that transcends nature (and so no immanent presence of transcendence, either). *Theological* naturalism goes one step further and concludes that nature should be the proper focus of human life, and everything that is humanly significant can be understood in terms of nature.

Now theologies can have quite various gods. If the gods are located in nature, what results is some sort of nature-religion, whether candid or not. It may be like the ancient polytheism or the shamanism that is the first known religion in every part of the world. Or it may be nominally "Christian," but a kind of Christianity that forces God to act in nature like any other natural cause.

As fascinating as shamanism is, let's stick with theological naturalism of a nominally Christian kind. This sort of naturalism assumes that *immanence* can only work by pushing aside a part of the *intramundane* to make room for the immanent presence of transcendence. (The idea of pushing things in this world aside to make room for the presence of transcendence comes from Robert Sokolowski, in *The God of Faith and Reason*.) Something can be an immanent presence, or it can be intramundane, but it can't be both at once. I don't know why people think this way, but they often do. It is a very naturalistic way to think. (It comes instinctively in the modern world.)

Clearly the comic strips and TV advertisements don't work this way, for we do not take the comics or TV ads literally. If we did, we would ask whether Mr. Clean *really* comes up out of the kitchen sink in a burst of light and sparkles. We would ask whether buying a Toyota Camry V-6 *really* will get you a better job and lots of glamour. We don't. There, we understand how language works.

And we have seen that there are lots of other problems with naturalistic explanations when we try to apply them even to human actions. For a naturalistic explanation is presumably unique, and once you have the one true naturalistic explanation, nothing more can be added to it. But the actions of the kid cruising on a summer evening are not like this. Narrative is the better kind of explanation for human actions, for it tells more than physics can, and it is open in ways that physics can never be.

One can find in Saint Augustine's *City of God* (around the year 430) places where he talks as if a human intention or a human will is the cause of the motions of the resulting human action. Twelve hundred years later, the sense of "cause" changed, and the human will becomes a *physical* cause of the motions of human actions. And here the problems start. For the physical motions of human actions, like raising an arm or hitting a ball (when human actions even *have* physical motions; the don't always) can't be traced back to anything *physical* that we could call a "will" or a "self." And so some people assumed that there is an *un*-physical human self or soul that exerts physical causes on the human body. This dodge hasn't done much better. Present day cognitive science is romping through the remains of such nonsense, having a field-day in its victory over "folk" psychology. And divine action pretty much went the way of human action, a hundred years earlier.

So where are we, how far have we come? We have seen how what really matters to us about human actions can't be explained in naturalistic terms. We can see what a naturalistic basic life orientation would be. For naturalism, all things are either determined or completely and essentially random, and there is nothing else, and no other kinds of explanation are allowed. All things humanly significant are forced to speak such a language. At least in "public," when we are being "official" and speaking on the record. After hours, when we read the comics, we don't notice that we don't think in naturalistic terms.

And when the sons of history are asked to sing a song of history on the alien soil of naturalism, what comes out is cause laundering. That's the only way to make history work in the land of nature. But no longer is it really a song of history.

4.2   God's Driver's License

Cause laundering is only the latest scheme to sneak God into the workings of nature. Traditionally, it has been done by what were called "miracles." It is only in the modern world that the miracle texts in the Bible were reinterpreted as "exceptions to natural laws," and it is not entirely clear how they were read before the modern period. When action has to work within natural laws, cause laundering is the inevitable mechanism. When action (divine action, at least) can make exceptions to natural laws, things are much easier, and cause laundering is not required. How miracles work will tell us a lot about how the religion of history thinks when it lives on the soil of naturalism. (Actually, it grew up on the soil of naturalism. In its original form, in the Exodus, it was a mutation of naturalistic religion, but that is well ahead of our story.)

Miracles are (or were) supposed to be the basis for faith. Their character as exceptions to natural laws supposedly certifies them as the basis for faith. There are too many hidden assumptions here, and it will take some work to unpack them. Supposedly, the anomalous events are acts of God.

Consider one, the "Virgin Birth"; it supposedly certifies Jesus as "divine." (That this is a disastrously oversimplified Christology, at least by the standards of theology in the fourth and fifth centuries, doesn't matter here. It is a fair approximation to much popular theology.)

The first problem is that it is impossible to say *what* happened: how did he get born without a human father? If the conception process was within the known laws of nature, then there is no miracle, and the events of his birth cannot be used to certify faith. If they are outside the known laws of nature, then as a practical matter, we do not know what happened. It would be extremely odd (to say the least) to try to rest a religion on events that are unknown and unknowable. It will not do to wave the hands and say that somehow the molecules just rearranged themselves—in something that anomalous, this is insufficient. Strong claims require stronger evidence than what we have in the virgin birth texts.

Which brings us to the second problem: assuming that one could hazard a hypothesis as to *what* happened, how is one to come to a historical judgement *that* it happened? Since certainty is impossible, and confidence decreases with implausible events, it would (once again) be extremely odd to base anything of value, such as the shape of human lives today, on historical conclusions that are as shaky as any conclusion to biological anomalies in Jesus's conception and birth must be. Those who would suspend the canons of historical judgement in order to reach their favored "miracles" thereby destroy any basis they might have for ascertaining the particulars of other events in history, events when they need critical judgement in history.

A third problem arises. Suppose that Jesus had been born with six fingers. Were the texts to tell us this, we might responsibly believe them; such anatomical anomalies do occur with measurable frequency. The problem is this: why would such an anomaly have any theological significance? And if six fingers couldn't prove Jesus to be the messiah, then why should a virgin birth?

Van Harvey's summary in *The Historian and the Believer* is very much to the point. People who want miracles use one metaphysics for their weekday lives and another for their "religious" lives. The inconsistency is not innocent, as we shall see.

The New Testament itself has words to say about this craving for miracles: it denounces it. It is a desire for "signs and wonders," a kind of faith quite alien to what Jesus was looking for. The faith he sought in people was the faith willing to risk one's life and lose it, not an attitude waiting for the security and gratifications of "miracles." We see this in the attitudes of the people in George Burns's movie, *Oh God!*. Burns plays the role of God, and late in the movie has to convince some skeptics that he really is God. He tries card tricks, and when they are not impressed, he asks them, "What would convince you?" His authentication was in what he said, not in some external proofs.

When some of my students discovered that I was not reading the "miracle" texts literally, they protested. I pointed out to them that modern genres of literature use special effects in ways that audiences can apply to their own lives without in any way being troubled by non-literalness. Movies and TV advertisements do this all the time, as we have already noticed. I asked them why the Bible should be forbidden to use literary techniques for showing human life like it is, techniques that modern readers and viewers take for granted in other contexts. In other words, why shouldn't the Bible be allowed to speak to them in the terms of their own time, in their own language, with the story-telling techniques they were used to? They gasped in shock and horror. "Because it's sacred! Because it's holy!" When I asked what "sacred" or "holy" might mean, they just gave me That Look: the flared nose, the twisted lip, what one produces recoiling in horror on beholding an international conference of stinks and molds in a tupperware casserole too long in the back of the fridge.

Look at what the birth narratives say, if one takes them against the background assumption that there was an anonymous human father. The first conclusion is that Jesus was a bastard, an illegitimate child. The second is that Joseph and Mary were both generous of heart to an exceptional degree. Given Jesus's taste in friends as revealed in the Gospels, associating with sinners as he does, it would make sense for God to come as a bastard. It fits his style.

One might protest that this makes Jesus's birth a less-than-immaculate conception. But I ask, which is more believable, a physical anomaly in conception, or a teleological suspension of the ethical, in Kierkegaard's phrase, by which Mary could conceive with a man not her husband, yet remain sinless? If God can suspend laws (this is what the literalists allege), then why can he not suspend *moral* laws, something for which we *do* have some warrants in ordinary experience? If people choose the interpretation less likely on grounds of modern experience (a physical law was suspended and not a moral law) then we may ask, Why? Perhaps they wish to protect their own respectability, and for God to come as a bastard undermines that respectability. In a less embarrassing possibility, people yearn for a cluster of virtues that includes sexual purity, chastity, continence, and so on. Biological anomalies would both legitimate and objectivate that yearning. Objectivation is the engine of naturalism in theology, and this would be but one more instance. But objectivation is not only not necessary for faith, it misunderstands faith. Objectivation is certainly not necessary for the honoring of chastity or the other virtues of our Lord's Mother.

Actually, there is a simpler explanation for the Virgin Birth texts, as is by now well known. The Greek for virgin, *parthenos*, was the Septuagint translation of Isaiah 7, which in the Hebrew has "an *almah* shall conceive and bear a son," and it is this prophecy in Isaiah that the birth narratives invoke to make sense of Jesus's origins. The Septuagint was a Greek translation of the Common Documents (what Christians know as "Old Testament", and Jews simply as "the Bible"), made in about the year 200 BCE in Alexandria. It is not particularly literal, and the translators evidently assumed their looseness of language would not cause problems. Non-literal language can often say things that literal language cannot. While *parthenos* means virgin, if one is being strict, *almah* merely means young woman. And *parthenos* need not be interpreted strictly.

Now the birth narratives occur *only* in the Gospels of Matthew and Luke, neither the earliest gospels nor the earliest documents in the New Testament. Mark does not know this story, and it would be odd for him to leave it out if he had known. John, coming later, doesn't know, doesn't care, or doesn't believe. Paul (earlier) gives no hint of it, and if it mattered and if he had known, it would be odd to leave it out. The plausible simplest explanation is that Matthew and Luke read the Septuagint and mis-read *parthenos* literally, and then *deduced* what must have happened. They or their readers have filled in the rest of the "miraculous" interpretation. On one explanation, Jesus's conception was unexceptional and the quest for biological anomalies is based on a misreading. On the other, Jesus was illegitimate. Either way, God is pulling your leg. That, too, is his style.

We got into this way of reading the Bible as "miraculous" with the excuse that the Bible is different from other literature because it is "sacred." This is like claiming to have God's driver's license, proof that his checks won't bounce. And so, with the divine ID in hand, one no longer has any risk in taking his promises. But the Bible does not make challenge after challenge to its readers only to retract the risk of its challenges in a few "miracles." Treating the Bible as "sacred"

is a way to evade its message, de-claw its challenge, and domesticate
the transcendent in it, all in the most invulnerable strategy one could
devise: in the very act of claiming to respect its challenge.

None of this, by the way, should be used to impugn the reverence
traditionally accorded to Mary's virginity. Her virginity is about her
relations to other people and to God, not about the material circumstances of Jesus's conception. Her virginity doesn't need biological
anomalies. We revere her for a constellation of virtues most prominent
among which are humility, obedience, and chastity. Those virtues are
themselves at the service of the Incarnation. My first point has merely
been that the Incarnation (and with it, the Virgin Birth) are neither
certified by biological anomalies nor refuted by absence of biological
anomalies. The second point was that the historian has no responsible
basis for claiming that there were any biological anomalies, and the
theologian has no need of such a claim.

Only on assumptions of theological naturalism would biological
anomalies be either necessary or sufficient to prove anything about
Jesus. Naturalism is a commitment to understanding the human world
solely in naturalistic terms. Theological naturalism is a commitment to
understanding God's action in this world *solely* in naturalistic terms.
But if faith (and theology, bringing faith to language) are to find
some basis other than naturalism, that basis has to be in something
transcendent to the world, and not just a mere extension of the world.
Naturalism in science seems to be a necessary condition of doing
science at all; naturalism in theology seems to me to be perverse. But
science and theology do not have to think in the same terms.

4.3   Beyond Nature

People often think that if Biblical religion is incompatible with naturalism, then the only remedy is to have a supernatural, "exceptions to
natural laws," places where God can act miraculously. Naturalism in
philosophy is the thesis that nature is all there is, there is nothing more
than nature, nothing outside of nature. And this does appear to rule
out the sort of miraculous events the Bible talks about, because they

don't happen in the natural world as we know it today.

The supposed alternative to naturalism is supernaturalism. Allowing a supernatural gives God room enough to act, and this is supposedly a minimal requirement for Biblical religion to make sense, whether in its ancient or contemporary varieties. Supernaturalism is a way to get divine efficient causes into the world we live in, and the world we live in is just the natural world. Plausible as such a thesis is, I don't think it works.

Supernaturalism is just naturalism by other means. Supernaturalism is a super sort of naturalism, naturalism writ large. Forced to speak of God within the language of naturalism, theology does so— and supernaturalism results. But the real alternative to naturalism is history. History goes well beyond nature, but does not contradict it. Transcendence is visible in history (as it is in nature, at a lower level) but its immanent presence does not disturb the normal workings of nature or history.

Maybe it would help to look at how the language of naturalism works, and how the several kinds of language in history work by contrast. Each has a kind of responsibility, but they are very different kinds of responsibility. The language of naturalism, at least today, abstracts from human involvements, it leaves human concerns out. The languages of history (and there are more than one) focus precisely on the human involvements, human concerns.

When we ask about the motions of natural bodies, all we want to know are the natural causes. That means a certain kind of efficient causes and material causes, causes that obey strict laws and always produce their effects. Often we want causes that can be described mathematically. We want causes that are *unique*, causes that are not open to multiple interpretations. In history, multiple interpretations are allowed, but not in science. And in the natural sciences, responsibility means leaving human concerns out of the description of nature and producing a description that other people can verify or observe in their own laboratories.

In history, by contrast, we ask quite different sorts of questions. In fact, there are (at least) two ways of approaching history, each with its characteristic questions and its own characteristic kind of responsibility. I think the difference is like the difference between a first-person account and a third-person account. In a third-person account, the one telling the story (the historian) is not taking responsibility for the actions he tells, but only for the truthfulness of the story he tells. In first-person history, the one telling the story takes responsibility for both, for the story *and* for the actions it tells. These two kinds of history work a little differently. When we listen to first-person history, we want to know what the events *meant* for the people who experienced them and for the people who identify with those historical actors after the fact, now, in the present. In third-person history, it would be true but not entirely helpful to say that we want to know "just the facts, please, just the facts." The two kinds of history can become confused, mixed, as when we ask the kid on a summer evening, "were you cruising?" If we are involved in the events, as family or friends (or police, God forbid), the texture can shift from third to first-person history easily.

In third-person history, we want to know how much one event has influenced others. In first-person history, we want to know the worth of an event, its value for the people involved. In third-person history, time is quantitative, a matter of dates and sequences. In first-person history, past time is present in the lives of people now. It is a matter of personal experience, but it is shared in a community, and so it does not have the capriciousness that we don't like when we call something "subjective."

I could go on, but these are fair examples of the differences. For those who relish a challenge, H. Richard Niebuhr's *The Meaning of Revelation* (1940) will provide many happy hours of reading. That book is my source, and it has some problems, but I have no intention of debugging it here.

One noticeable difference between third-person history, "external" history, "they" history, and first-person history, "internal" or "we" history, is that "we" history often uses figurative language to show how things felt or what they meant in the lives of people then and now. External history tends to be much more sparing (and much more

careful) of such language. We can read an internal history and more
or less reconstruct what an external history of the same events would
look like. People do this with the internal accounts of history in both
the Common Documents and the New Testament.

Sometimes these literary devices are what we would today call
"special effects." How the stories arose in the first place is a question
for Biblical scholars, and not always an easy one to answer. The
Biblical texts usually make it clear that the kind of responsibility they
are after is that of a first-person narrative, one person's challenge to
the life and lifestyle of another, and not the third-person responsibility
to the "facts" of an external historian.

Special effects, whether in the Bible, in movies, or in advertisements, work to make visible what would otherwise be invisible. They
show how it felt to experience the events, what it was like to be changed
by the events. Because they show what it was like to be *changed* by
the events, one can hardly dismiss them as "subjective" in the sense
of "making it up," reading things into the events that were not "really"
there. They tell us what the Israelites experienced in the Exodus and
the Exile. They tell us what the Church and the Synagogue experienced
in the disasters of the first century.

These texts have been changed in the modern world. What were
literary devices to explain the subjective experience of events that
were very objective have become something quite different. (Little
Judah was, after all, very objectively carried off into Babylon, and
very much against its will.) The responsibility implicit in the texts
has been shifted. It was an *avowal* of an experience, and undertaking
of responsibility for an experience in the past and for its implications
in the present. It has become (for the modern world) a *report* of
a phenomenon, precisely as naturalistic language abstracts from and
hides human involvements. The emphasis of the stories in both the
Common Documents and in the New Testament has been radically
changed. A people in history has been eclipsed, and what used to
be the story of its life has become mere "evidence" for God. In the
Common Documents, prophets' warnings about the (then) near future
have been turned into predictions of events long after. In the New

Testament, the "miracle" stories have become the preternatural events that work as God's Driver's License.

The responsibility *for the experiences* has now been shifted. For the physical phenomena, observable in naturalistic terms, are now supposed to take the responsibility for the experience. That experience and its accompanying commitments are no longer avowed. One need no longer answer Jesus's question (just to take the Christian side of the problem), "Who do you say that I am?", openly and candidly. We no longer hear "Who do *you* say that I am?", nor do we feel the discomfort of being put on the spot. Instead, we think we can answer with, "You said you were so-and-so", or "We know from the miracles that you are such-and-such."

The special effects were a way of externalizing something that was internal and existential, personal, a matter of lived experience. Externalization is a literary way of making the invisible and internal visible for other people. But what was externalized figuratively has been taken literally, and now what was externalized and taken literally has become objectivated. What is objective and treated in objective language is separated and divorced from human avowal, human re- sponsibility. The people who have allowed this to happen to their language have been alienated from the events and the history that was supposed to be the center of their lives.

Chapter 5

History, You Say?!

5.1   The History of History

Since I make such a big deal about history, it might help to look at the history of history, or rather, the history of history-*writing*. It has changed some since the seventeenth century, and a lot since the ancient world. The best example of "internal" history from the ancient world is probably the story in the books of Joshua, Judges, Samuel, and Kings. This story was in all probability put together by one editor, who also produced the book of Deuteronomy, and so it is known as the Deuteronomic History. This history is the core history in the Common Documents, and it is fairly clear in its focus on the consequences for the lives of those who inherit it. It is first-person history. We shall come to it in due time. There were other internal histories, cited often in 1 and 2 Kings: the Annals of the Kings of Israel and the Annals of the Kings of Judah. But these books are lost to us. External history can be found in the few places that notice Israel and Judah in the annals of their conquerors.

History looks a lot different today from how it looked one or two hundred years ago. It is not just that there has been a gigantic cleaning of all the closets in the world, finding myriad documents that were lost or forgotten. Once found, the documents were read in a different light. Beyond documents, there has been a lot of digging; ruins of thousands of cities, large and small, have been excavated. Starting with Troy and Babylon and the Pyramids, entire civilizations have been reconstructed that were buried and known in only the foggiest memories.

But there has been a deeper change in how history is understood. Some of the change comes from the light of science, but some of the change happened *before* the modern sciences got started. The little word "critical" has been used to describe the change in attitude, for people began to ask themselves, "do I really believe these texts?" and "could what the texts say really have happened?"

There was a famous document giving land to the Popes, allegedly a deed written by the Emperor Constantine, in the fourth century. It attracted suspicion in the fifteenth century, and was eventually exposed as a forgery. More interesting were the grounds for thinking it a forgery: the style and language of the text, the terminology used, and incongruous references to the history and legal codes.

Changes in historical thinking accelerated after the sciences got started. With the sciences came a faith that the world is orderly in a physical sense, a faith grounded in a larger faith in the sovereignty of God, who ordained the natural laws that the natural world obeys. It was that faith that enabled the sciences to get going at all, for without it, the natural world was presumably disorderly, fantastic and enchanting, but not something that could be studied or understood.

The miracle texts attracted suspicion early, but they were not the best clues to the new understanding of biblical history. To be sure, they came under attack in the eighteenth century, but that attack ended in a stalemate, with believers and skeptics unable to do much to each other. It was not the skeptics, but a few faithful scholars who unraveled the way the Bible was put together.

In the 1700s, a few people began to notice peculiar things in the first five books of the Bible, traditionally attributed to Moses. They surmised that Moses used multiple sources in composing these five books. Some of the tell-tale evidence was the fact that different texts in Genesis and Exodus use different names for God, but there are plenty of other clues as well. A century later, this was to become the "Documentary Hypothesis," the thesis that the Pentateuch passed through at least four successive editions (none by Moses), and each editor contributed his own characteristic language and theology. (They are known by letters, J, E, D, and P, and the theory has acquired a nickname, "JEDP.") In the eighteenth century, scholars suspected that Mark (and not Matthew) was the first Gospel. They guessed that Matthew and Luke read Mark, rearranged what they saw, and added new material. In one form or another, this has remained the majority opinion since then.

In the nineteenth century, biblical criticism came into its own. The composition and editing of most of the Common Documents were reconstructed. In the Gospels, things were somewhat rockier, because the churches, both officially and popularly, were sensitive and touchy about revising the received traditional interpretations. Many scholars tried to synthesize "lives of Jesus." Such projects in hindsight were invariably failures, for they produced images of Jesus that merely made him look like one or another nineteenth-century ideal (usually Liberal). Nevertheless, the effort was not fruitless, for its failure brought significant lessons. Jesus as a first-century figure stands out after Jesus the nineteenth-century Liberal is no longer credible. And people realized that the Gospels are not biographies, and are not what I have called "external" history, disinterested "facts." They *contain* internal history, but they *are* advertisements, and they intend to solicit a change of life from their readers and hearers.

In parallel to the exploration of sacred history interest in wider secular history grew also. At first, historians thought that it was possible to get to the facts "as they actually were." As the century progressed, they devised new ways of sifting and testing evidence.

The English have written a lot of history, and indeed cherish and treasure their own history as few other peoples do. But for the English, history-*writing* has usually been a fairly straightforward affair. It was the Germans who watched themselves as they wrote. They were fussy about "method," the kind and order of questions they asked. They noticed that whenever they were studying Papal or Turkish or French or British history, they were also thinking about their own history, and about applications in their own time. They began to suspect that what they knew of the past depended largely on their own questions in the present.

This condition has a name; it is called "historical relativity." The Enlightenment of the 1700s considered history to be a problem and historical relativity even more of a problem. The Enlightenment sought to place its confidence in timeless truths of reason rather than contingent (and dubious) conjectures about history. It did not like history.

And the historians of the nineteenth century began with an Enlightenment optimism that real knowledge of historical "facts" was possible after all. But as the century progressed, they revised their understanding of truth in history, and then ended by seriously revising the Enlightenment optimism itself.

It is not as if they knew less than before. They clearly knew more, a lot more. They understood the ancient world (from which and on whose soil they had grown up) in ways that previous centuries never did. Rome stood out in a clarity as never before. Early Christian history likewise.

It was as if they had discovered that every historical actor in the ancient world was like our seventeen-year old on an August Friday evening. Was he recharging the battery, avoiding a quarrel, avoiding homework, going to the store, cruising, or just escaping the heat? That depends on whether you (the "historian"!) are the brother, the father, the mother, the girl-friend, or the family dog.

What someone was doing in the past depends on how it affects your life in the present. Put a little differently, you only get answers to questions that you actually ask, and you can only ask questions that arise from your life in the present.

5.2   Ernst Who?!

It gets worse. It is as if you (the historian, again) are not sure whether you are the brother, the mother, the girl-friend, or the dog, or some actor who has yet to appear on the stage. (Klingon historians visiting the remains of an ancient earth?) Most likely the last.

These things came together as a smoldering crisis in the obscure figure of Ernst Troeltsch. Well might one ask, Ernst Who?, because he is not much known outside history and theology departments, and not always well known even there. His picture, the picture that appeared on the front of a recent biography of him, looks surprisingly like the actor Jack Nicholson in one of his more evil roles. My students tell me that I am delusional, but I still maintain that a make-up artist would have very little work to do on Mr. Nicholson to make him look like the picture of Professor Troeltsch. (The problem is that Nicholson is usually photographed smiling, and Troeltsch was serious in the only photograph I've seen. And Troeltsch had more hair.)

Be all that as it may, Troeltsch (pronounced "Treltsch," rhymes with Welch) has been something of an evil figure in the world of the Christian faithful. It is as if Troeltsch were the grinch who stole Christmas—and all the rest of the Gospel history, one event after another. I think this is a shame, because once you get around the confusions that he inherited from the Enlightenment, what is left is a historian's vision of unusual clarity and faith. It is not a sentimental or comforting faith, but it is nevertheless a faith in the truth, even when the truth hurts.

For Troeltsch, it hurt, and he died without resolving the problems that he inherited from the Enlightenment. He did not find a constructive way to live with the historical method he felt duty-bound to embrace, a way of doing historical research that he understood better than any of his contemporaries. It was also a method that he felt was hostile to the Christian faith he inherited at the same time.

It would be ironic if the appearance of hostility between Christianity and honesty in history were how things really stand. I don't think it is, and with a little effort, it is possible to show that Troeltsch's questions reflect a commitment that is more faithful to the roots of biblical religion than was the "orthodoxy" of his time. That is a long story, a little too long for this book, but some hints of it can be given here.

Ernst Troeltsch was born in 1865 in Augsburg, a city in southern Germany. He died in 1923, just before a series of lectures planned for England that he did not live to deliver himself. His teaching and writing began in 1891, first in theology, and then philosophy, with an emphasis on philosophy of history and its implications for theology. He stood at the crossings of many movements.

First among them was German Liberal theology. Liberal theology was notorious for its dislike of any kind of supernatural. It was also very suspicious of any kind of transcendence. And it tolerated historical research only because it didn't care much about history, trusting instead in general principles that it thought independent of history. In this suspicion of history, it followed the Enlightenment's dislike of history. Liberal Theology has also attracted a reputation for abandoning essential features of Christian theology. In Troeltsch's case, I suppose there is some truth in this, inasmuch as when he asked himself what was left of Christianity worth saving, his answer was just "Europeanism," a religion to promote European culture.

Secondly, Troeltsch inherited an Enlightenment craving for absolute religious knowledge, independent of any historical or contingent circumstances. Every form of relativity was rejected by the Enlightenment, on the tacit assumption that if absolute knowledge is not available, then only nihilistic relativism is left. (This does not make sense, but people do think this way just the same.)

Third, Troeltsch inherited the consciousness of historical relativity that came from the historians themselves, as we saw in the last section. There was a growing awareness of the historian's role in shaping the story that he tells. That awareness could only create enormous anxieties about the certainty of historical knowledge and about the responsibility of the historian who creates it. Those anxieties are still with us today.

I think I can draw out of Troeltsch's philosophy of history a theology that is more orthodox than the "Europeanism" that he thought himself left with. We can start with what Troeltsch did see, rather than what he did not see. He recognized the problem of the relativity of all human knowledge and action to one's own particular time and place. He understood the logic of a historian's thinking as few had before, though I think he missed parts of it. He knew that rigorous historical thinking was incompatible with the then-traditional "orthodoxy," an orthodoxy of "miracles," events that "prove" divine intervention in history. And he believed in the truth, even when the truth hurt. Does the truth do you any good, when the truth hurts? Troeltsch believed that it brings good, even though he could not see how.

Troeltsch knew he could not defend any absoluteness for Christianity. He both disliked relativity and knew that it is a fact of life. We see only from where we stand, not from some point outside of history. At the end of his career, he reluctantly embraced a *confessional* stance instead of seeking *proof* for the correctness of his own religion. In a confessional stance, you accept relativity and simply confess your faith in your own time and place. How that confession is to transcend time and place without turning into delusions of absoluteness is a puzzle for later.

What Troeltsch is most famous for are the features of a historian's thinking known in a series as "criticism, analogy, and correlation."

Criticism means that the historian always functions as a critic of the evidence he finds, and his results are always open to criticism by other people. Moreover, his interpretation of that evidence is always merely probable, it never achieves absolute certainty. People who want certainty, and who want to base it on external history, will reject Troeltsch at this point also. But there are other kinds of certainty, and other ways to get it.

Analogy just means that you (the historian) have no business claiming to know anything about alleged events in the past for which there are strictly zero analogies in the present. This rules out "miracles"—if the miracle texts are taken as reports of physically anomalous events. You can see why Troeltsch was again not welcome in "orthodox" circles. At least not in orthodoxy as the nineteenth century conceived it. But we have already seen that miracles, used as God's Driver's License, are neither necessary nor sufficient to ground faith.

The last feature of the historian's method was known as *correlation*. What the principle of correlation says is that explanation in history has to be in terms of other historical actors—and not God. This is the counterpart for history of the rule that God is not an explanation in the natural sciences. But this is *external* history. Troeltsch and many since him have not been very clear about the differences and relations between external and internal history. Internal history, the telling of a story for which one takes a kind of responsibility that is excluded from external history, can legitimately speak in analogies that are forbidden to external history. God is one of those analogies, *if* you understand how such analogies work.

Clearly, Troeltsch's approach to history can seem unwelcome. It appears to offer cold comfort for "orthodoxy." I think that appearance will change, because Troeltsch's central commitments are more orthodox than the "orthodoxy" of the nineteenth century. Consider criticism, analogy, and correlation in turn.

First, criticism. Why should I use a historical method that is sloppy or corrupt on the history that I really care about, when I routinely demand rigorous historical research on less important events? And how can "orthodoxy" get away with opposing the truth? The fact that the truth can hurt or mean less than total and absolute certainty shouldn't make any difference. Either "orthodoxy" was not worth much, or orthodox Christianity was misunderstood. I think it was misunderstood, as we shall see.

Next, analogy. The criterion of analogy is more flexible than one might think. You can construct a chain of analogies, getting from the present to the past in many small steps. It is not necessary to find the past to be "just like" the present in every respect. Clearly, much or most of the past has been quite unlike the present, and saying that doesn't require any "miracles" at all. But the criterion of analogy is one of the ways we sift the possible from the impossible. Without it, we are left helpless. To ask for exceptions in one place (when it is convenient) and to use it strictly in another place (again, when it is convenient) is just corrupt historical research.

Last, correlation. I think correlation is easily misunderstood. It is largely a matter of keeping straight what kind of questions one is asking, and at different times, you can ask very different kinds of questions about the past. On one occasion, you just want to know what intramundane historical causes came together in such-and-such an event, and for the moment, you have no stake in the events, or you want to ignore your own stake in the events. Here, God is not allowed as an explanation, precisely because the *question* is not about God, but about intelligible intramundane connections between events of a historical kind.

On another occasion, what you really want to know is precisely what's in it for you, what your stake in the events is, who you identify with, who the heroes are. Here, God is allowed as an explanation, because God is often the best way to say what the experience of history "from inside" is like. That assumes that you believe in God. As we saw early, the choice between Fate, fortune, and divine action as explanation for physically random events is not one that can be made from within the physical sciences. It cannot be determined from "external" history either.

We now have two kinds of uncertainty. Human knowledge in history is relative to the time and place of the knower. And the interpretation of it (in terms of God or some other ultimate causes) appears to be a matter of choice. We are left with a sense of anxiety, maybe a sense of falling, of having no support.

5.3 Right Here in Liver City

Perhaps an example will help. Once upon a time, right here in Livermore, a miracle happened. In my house. Now a miracle is supposed to be a violation of a natural law, and this one certainly qualifies. It was a violation of Gauss's law. And it happened in my bathroom, in the shower.

We can skip the mathematics. Gauss's law just says that if you want to go from the inside of a closed surface to the outside of that closed surface, you have to actually go *through* the closed surface. I could set up closed surfaces all I liked (plastic garbage bags and duct-tape are very useful here), but I couldn't for the life of me see how the water was getting from the shower head to the outside, to the bathroom floor. So I declared it to be a miracle.

Alas, the miracle ceased when the bathroom was rebuilt with a new floor and a new shower.

Now you may complain. But think about it, for if you do complain, you are treading the path that Mr. Troeltsch trod many decades ago.

If you doubt what I say, if you ask yourself whether Porter might be pulling your leg, you are admitting the possibility of the very thing I've been saying about the miracle texts in the Bible.

If you ask yourself whether I might have corrupt motives (or just any motives at all) for telling you this story, you are exercising the function of *criticism*, just as Mr. Troeltsch suggested you should. And you are admitting that there is less than complete certainty in the interpretation of the miracle text above.

If you look for some standards by which to judge that text—such as asking whether such things as violations of Gauss's law actually do happen, you are exercising the historian's criterion of *analogy*.

Suppose you decide there *was* a violation of Gauss's law. The water went from the shower head to the bathroom floor without traversing a continuous path of points in between. If you now ask yourself whether God had anything to do with this event, you have already posed the question in a naturalistic way, and you have to confront the matter of *correlation*. If you rule out such "divine action" on principle, even on a principle of limited and local application to this particular event, you have bought into Mr. Troeltsch once again.

If you apply Troeltsch's criteria selectively, then on what principle do you choose when to use them, and when to suspend them? If you are selective, I can always reply, "If you won't believe in my miracles, I don't have to believe in your miracles." It's much easier to be consistent.

And what about the theological significance of this violation of Gauss's law? Is it without any theological significance? Don't be hasty and go jumping to conclusions! I can sing my heart out in the shower, doing the *Salve Regina* to make the saints weep. Maybe that caused the violation of Gauss's law. Maybe it was a *negative* miracle: God put the puddle on the bathroom floor because he couldn't stand that godawful catterwalling.

But how would you know?

5.4   Wraiths of Deneb and Rigel

Our sun is a modest star, even though it is about a hundred times the diameter of the earth. (And ten times the diameter of Jupiter, which is intermediate in size.) Astronomers call it a G2 star, which means that it is slightly yellow in color, and of an ordinary magnitude. In fact, its mass is taken as the standard unit of stellar mass. It is a very ordinary star, one of countless many more like it. About five billion years old or a little more, it is in the middle of its life-cycle.

Some stars are much, much larger. They can extend out as far as the orbit of Mercury, or even almost to the orbit of Mars (as Betelgeuse does). They may be cooler or hotter than the sun. Sometimes near the surface of one of these stars, there are micro-fluctuations in the stellar gas. Those fluctuations can be correlated with one another, and their correlations are a way of encoding information. Pretty soon, and this fantasy will have a self-sentient life form in the upper atmosphere of such a star. In effect, the star itself is alive. (Freeman Dyson, great physicist that he is, did not hesitate to imagine more bizarre life-forms than this one, and he published in the refereed technical literature.) Explore with me what such a life-form would be like. It does not really know matter cooler than about 3000 degrees (for a red giant star), or cooler than 10,000 degrees (for a white supergiant). It does not have any experience of what we would call "un-ionized" gas, gas in which all the electrons are attached to atoms or molecules. In such stars, the gas is always partially ionized, with a lot of electrons ripped off their atoms and screaming around free by themselves. Ionized gas is called plasma in the astronomy business. Living beings made of diaphanous gas are called wraiths in the fantasy business. So these life-forms could be called "plasma-wraiths" of the upper atmospheres of giant stars.

Such a life-form would of course have no experience of the liquid state and all the myriad complexities that *we* know in living liquids such as water-based living cells on earth. (Water may be more important for life here than even carbon!) And such a living star could have no knowledge of solid bodies. If we could talk to it, it would have extreme difficulty understanding what we are like.

Nevertheless, it would have some concept of death, and with mortality, a concept of finiteness of lived time. It would have some equivalent of worry about what to do with its remaining time. So there would be a few things in common, and a lot that is not in common. They would have knowledge, of a sort, and since they can send electromagnetic waves to each other, they can communicate.

Now thinkers of the Enlightenment in the eighteenth century (to return to earth) thought that they could attain knowledge that is absolute, valid for all times and all places—and presumably for all knowers. Even the plasma-wraiths of Deneb and Rigel, two supergiant stars prominent in our sky. But the idea that they could understand (for example) the pythagorean theorem, the basis of much of our geometry, in the same way that we do, seems wildly reckless. That they would even understand counting as we do seems dubious. That they could understand Picasso well enough to like (or even dislike) his work seems unlikely. Mozart, on the other hand, is conceivable—but not as we understand his music. Music is possible for beings made of plasma, for they are in a sense made of sound-waves.

This is preposterous. It is not necessary to do philosophy or science or history for the plasma-wraiths of giant stars. They may have problems, but their problems are not our problems. Five hundred years ago, you would have told me that I do not even have to solve the problems of Chinese civilization (to take an example closer to home). I only need to know what to do next in my own time and my own culture.

In other words, relative knowledge, if it really is knowledge, is sufficient. To know what to do next, relative to one's own culture, is enough. To understand the world, relative to one's own standpoint, is enough. If it really is knowledge, and not confusion, knowledge and not error, it is enough.

So there should not be a problem with "relativity," as I have defined it. What people *call* relativity is another matter entirely. And they usually mean moral relativity and not knowledge-of-the-world relativity, because moral relativity is a lot easier to understand. We have some experience of it, after all, when two cultures meet and disagree on basic moral standards. What people usually mean by (moral) relativity is in fact more like nihilistic relativ*ism*, the thesis that there are *no* standards of right and wrong. This is quite different from saying that there *is* a (relative) standard of right and wrong, one that will tell me what to do next in my own culture and my own time.

People jump to the conclusion that there are no moral standards for several reasons. Probably the simplest is the fact that when two cultures come in contact and disagree, there is often no easy or simple way to resolve the disagreement. That does not mean there is no (hard) way to resolve the disagreement, just that it is not simple or easy. I think there is a deeper reason, and that is that people would like to think their knowledge and their moral standards are valid in all times and all places. This—notwithstanding the fact that their own sacred texts record moral standards in their own tradition (polygamy, for only one example) that they would today consider extremely offensive!

Less often than culture contact is culture confusion, the dis-integration of a culture's moral vision, breakup into sub-cultures. People live side by side with moral differences that go deeper and deeper. Moral confusion and the inability to sort it out are the experience that gets called "relativism." People can respond with "nihilism," the thesis that nothing means anything in the end, and in the meanwhile, the only things that matter are my own desires. Here there is a sort of relativity, but it is relativity to self, to caprice, to whimsy, to self-indulgence. It is relativity to one's sub-culture. It happens when there are no plausible community standards. "Relativity" (to caprice and whimsy) is *lack* of relativity to community standards. It means *not* knowing what to do next in one's own time and place.

Nevertheless, people want "something more" than just to know what to do here and now. Culture contact (with external cultures) and culture confusion (internal to a culture) expose moral standards as something human beings make, not written in the stars. If you *thought* that only standards "written in the stars" (also known as "objective" standards) could really be "true," then of course there is no moral truth. Nihilism is an understandable response.

But look at what follows if human moral standards are a product

of human history. It follows that people are *responsible* not just for
their actions, but also for the standards by which their actions are
judged. This invites anxiety. Major anxiety. You are left holding the
bag, not just for your actions, but for the standards you are judged
by. At some level, people would like to believe in truth. At least at
the level of exposure: the idea that, somewhere, somehow, at least in
principle, other people can see what you are doing. And wanting a
moral standard but not having one, trying to act by a moral standard
that has no visible "objective" support is one first-class way to feel
lonely, exposed, vulnerable. It is easy to want out of responsibility,
out of anxiety.

So people want *still* something more. What would satisfy people
is a sense that they have at least *something* beyond the mere here and
now, beyond what to do *just* relative to our own time and place. If
we are limited to knowledge relative to our own time and place, what
could transcend that limitation without contradicting it?

How can human knowledge reach beyond the limitations of historical relativity without being in denial about historical relativity? The
answer to that question comes in two parts. The first (and easiest) is
about how to live well *within* historical relativity, how to be responsible. That we come to next. The hard part is about the analogies we
live by, the analogies we think with. It is those analogies that can reach
beyond historical relativity in this world without denying it. That we
will come to only in the end of the book. Begin with how to live well
within historical relativity, how to be responsible. Then we can see
how historical religion actually works.

5.5   The Cat's Away

Ernst Troeltsch could be pardoned for his discouragement. In all
fairness, he did not have the tools to make sense of historical relativity.
He could not see how people live responsibly with relativity. In one
form or another, the problem of historical relativity has dogged the
twentieth century. It has colored most of philosophy, ethics, and
theology. Help, as it turns out, comes from ethics, in the work of

Alasdair MacIntyre. He is a Scottish philosopher who migrated from Britain to the United States and made a complicated pilgrimage from occasional half-Marxism in his early career to a theory of virtue much like Aristotle's in his mature thinking. But it is an Aristotelian ethics with a strong sense of history.

Unlike most thinkers in ethics who dread history (thinking it is only confusion, with no promise of real help), MacIntyre actually read the history of ethics (and wrote a book on it, too). Not one to deny the hard times that virtue ethics has fallen on, he called the book that made his reputation *After Virtue*, as if to say, "Here's how we got to where we are now, what do we do next?" Several books later, his friends responded with a collection of essays in his honor called *After MacIntyre*. But the thesis was stated in a nutshell in the title of the book after *After Virtue*, namely, *Whose Justice? Which Rationality?*

That is the problem, isn't it? Which rationality? Which standard do we live by, in making sense of things? For there are multiple and competing standards. MacIntyre's problem is ethics, and he traces the major traditions in ethical thinking from their roots to the present. Our problem is bigger than ethics, but MacIntyre's reflections can be transferred from ethics to any situation where multiple traditions encounter and compete. MacIntyre's problem arose from a great confusion of multiple traditions in ethical thought. We have already seen the crisis in historical thinking in the person of Ernst Troeltsch. MacIntyre borrowed from the historians to solve his problems in ethics.

As it happens, MacIntyre borrowed from history of science rather than directly from the German historians, but it all comes down to about the same thing. History of science was faced with the problem of relativity as every other area of philosophy has been in the twentieth century. Thomas Kuhn in 1960 pulled together the suggestions of several philosophers before him into a more or less coherent synthesis. It was not entirely a stable synthesis, and has been the site of a lot of wrangling since then, but Kuhn's thesis permanently changed the shape of history and philosophy of science. (It was Thomas Kuhn who borrowed the term "paradigm" and coined the term "paradigm shift" to explain scientific revolutions.) His ideas show up in slightly more developed form in MacIntyre. They had, in effect, found the way to solve the problems that Troeltsch could not.

What happens in an encounter between two traditions? To put the question at its hardest, what happens when two traditions bump into each other and have a hard time talking to each other? When it is hard to translate from one to the other? If you can just translate the language of one into the language of the other, then they really are not very different traditions, they just have different (but equivalent) names for things. But what if you *can't* translate, because the two traditions are really different in the way they think? Then what?

Even if you can't translate, you *can* learn to think in both traditions. (You have to do that before you can even realize that simple translation is impossible!) At this point, some comparisons are possible, even if translation is not. Any tradition in philosophy or religion or ethics or one of the sciences will have unfinished business, problems it is still working on. And it will have explanations for its own unsolved problems. Here is where comparison is possible. For each tradition may *also* explain the *other* tradition's unsolved problems. Sometimes one tradition can even solve the other tradition's problems, not just explain them. In effect, each tradition is a standpoint from which it is possible to compare the traditions. And one standpoint may work better than the other. Or it may be possible to combine them in a synthesis. At this point, the observer is entitled rationally to choose between traditions. This is what rationality is, in the choice between traditions.

Within a tradition, rationality is also historical. It is a matter of knowing the history of the tradition and its problems up until the present. In other words, rationality means being a well-informed partner in its continuing conversation, able to advance the tradition according to its own standards of progress.

This is the solution that developed in the conversation in twentieth-century philosophy, as it looked at history, science, and ethics. People who read MacIntyre call it "tradition-bound rationality."

In effect, if you are a historical being whose life is inescapably relative to your own history, what you have is not absolute truth but responsibility. You *can* achieve responsibility. For it is possible to find out how conversations in philosophy or religion have come down to the present, and it is possible to continue them intelligently. Where multiple traditions come in contact, it is possible to come to rational comparisons between them, even if it takes a lot of work.

Such a comparison does not seek a standpoint outside of both traditions, and thus it does not deny historical relativity. But it can, in its own peculiar way, reach beyond the circumstances of its own time and place.

How would you state a claim that can reach beyond your own time and place? When you can see only your own time and place? It is a claim about other people, about other observers and what they would see if they could stand in your shoes. You claim that you have solved your own problems correctly. That is, on the terms posed by your own tradition, you claim a correct solution to your own tradition's next problems. More broadly, you claim that any observer who can understand your own tradition can see this. That observer may on the standards and explanations of *his* own tradition not agree—but he can see that on *your* standards, you got it right. This is not much, and by itself, it does not reach very far beyond the bare simple relativity of your own tradition and its problems. But it is a necessary start.

You do know more than this. You know (if past experience is any guide) that eventually, from the perspective of some other tradition, you will be found wrong. There will eventually be people who can explain your problems better than you can, and explain your successes and failures better than you can. In all probability, they will disagree on how to solve your problems. Reposed in their own terms, they will have what they think are better solutions.

Consider an example. Once upon a time, I had an argument with a graduate student in laser physics. He insisted that quantum electrodynamics was the most perfect theory known to physics. Predictions of physical quantities to twelve significant figures mean that QED (as it is known in the business) is not just the best theory we have, it is "true," absolutely. I asked him whether it would or could never be revised or overthrown, as classical mechanics had been, twice, once by relativity and once by quantum mechanics. At first, he actually said no. Then I put the question in personal terms: is this a theory that bars forever the progress of ambitious graduate students like yourself? Then he relented. Then he allowed that scientific progress might someday go beyond QED.

Yet there is a claim on behalf of QED, and of every other successful theory in the sciences, and it is a claim that goes well beyond the relative circumstances of time and place. It is a claim about the future generation, the one that will overthrow our current theories. That future generation will be able to understand our problems better than we do ourselves. To be sure, it will revise our solutions. But it will also be able to see where our solutions are indeed correct. For example, both relativity and quantum mechanics can say where classical mechanics, the old-fashioned Newtonian mechanics, gives correct answers. In a word, we do not dread being relativised, we expect to be relativised, and we expect to be vindicated in the very revisions that show us to be "wrong."

If this kind of thinking is allowed in the sciences, why is it not allowed in history, ethics and religion?

5.6   Want to Play Tennis?

If living with historical relativity is a matter of responsibility and not of absolute truth, how does responsibility work? The first thing to re-member is that responsibility is not a property, something that human beings might have, like brown or blond hair. It is not something that people might not have, like blue or green hair. It is an activity, and one that people participate in on a voluntary basis. You may be surprised by this claim. In some quarters, people think that you have to prove that human actions are not determined by natural causes before you can even talk about human freedom, and without human freedom, there can be no responsibility. This is the naturalist assumption. I shall defend my counter-claim not by addressing naturalism, but simply by observ-ing that the activity we call responsibility happens, and by laying out its features. Or rather, we may turn to the work of Herbert Fingarette, who has done this for us (1967, p. 34 ff.). Fingarette exhibits the basic contrasts in illustrating his contentions about responsibility as an activity. Let me paraphrase.

Imagine an attempted game. Have you ever tried to get some else to play with you, when there was nothing to do? Tennis, for example. Sometimes the other person is not really interested. Plead though you may, you won't get what you really want. Reluctantly, the other person gets his racquet. The game commences. And soon you notice that something is not quite right. He goes through all the motions, and he doesn't actually break any rules. But that's all. It's as if his racquet is too heavy to lift, it's a burden for him. He's not tired, but plays as if he were weary. He's not really into the spirit of the game. It's not worth much. Really, it's not worth much at all. He's just trying to get out of your pestering, just killing time until he can get back to what he was doing before. He appears to care, but does not. He may get the ball, if it comes to him, but he won't stretch for it if you hit it far enough to make it sporting. It may come back to you, it may just bounce out of bounds. Losses are just blah, wins get no sign of triumph. He won't make a serious effort. Why should he? He's just trying to satisfy the appearances because he has to. Did he ever really want to play? Did he ever understand what it meant to play?

The lot of those who have to deal with someone who is not responsible in real life is grim. As Fingarette says, they must endure the "exasperating, stupid, exhaustingly repetitious—and withal casual—character of the genuinely non-responsible" person (1967, p. 37). There is no recourse but to acquiesce, and to defend oneself, if need be, against the irresponsible one. There is no gallantry, no sportsmanship, no generosity, no feeling for other people, no virtue. And there are none of the vices we expect with real evil; there is no *effort* at evil. Real evil will put up a fight, real evil has a plan, real evil will challenge. But casual destructiveness is more typical of the truly irresponsible. Irresponsibility is banal.

It is the same with the asking and giving of reasons for human actions. Some are interested, some are not. Those who are not interested often don't even seem to know that such an activity is possible. For others, the activity, if it is entered at all, plays out by different rules than the rules of historical thinking.

It is pointless to hold responsible someone who will not play the game, who will not enter into the activity of responsibility. As Fingarette somewhere says, the irresponsible person may, through moral change, later *become* what he was not, a responsible person, and then accept responsibility for his past acts. But we can only appeal, and then only wait.

The activities of everyday life are where all these analogies come home. For people who think historically, the question "what was he doing?", when asked about our cruising teen-ager, makes sense. For naturalistic thinking, trying to figure out what he was doing, which of six or seven plausible stories his evening drive best fits into, isn't worth the effort. It doesn't matter. The bare physical motions suffice to answer the question, to tell what he was doing. No further intentions are acknowledged or admitted.

What is at stake in the activity of responsibility? When it is played "for real," as a kind of historical questioning about what has happened? The first thing that is at stake is the question of what people have done. What people have done determines what their obligations are. For people are responsible (if they are willing to play the game) for the consequences and implications of their actions. In the end, the participants themselves are at stake, for they have conceived their own lives, their own selves, in ways that are changed by the question of what they are doing, what they have done.

In history, whether it is grand history of a culture over centuries or individual history of a mere evening, the characterization of human actions is open in a way that the description of natural phenomena is not. We don't know all the possible narratives that an action can be fitted into. As the future unfolds, those possible narratives may change greatly. And so, in a sense, what has happened in the past can be changed in the future. For the narrative that was expected and intended may not be what actually happens. A harmless risk that would have been mere clowning if it had no consequences can become reckless or even criminal negligence if there are harmful consequences later on.

Some features of human action stand out (Niebuhr, 1963). Taking responsibility means recognizing these features, and acting on them. Actions are responses to situations and to prior actions, and they are intentional. That is, they proceed from interpretation of other people's prior acts. By contrast, knee-jerks are not actions, because they are not intentional.

The question of what is happening is itself a matter of interpretation, as we have had occasion to see already. The larger context for this question, by the way, always envisions the future as life-giving or death-dealing. Acts have consequences, for good or ill.

People are accountable. That is, people can explain what they were trying to do, and we expect them to explain if need be. People are expected to offer justifiable reasons for what they do. To a great extent, justification depends on the prior interpretation of the actions. (Going to the store to get bread and milk may be justifiable, where cruising was not.)

In a word, action takes place in a context of conversation, for conversation is always possible to clarify what people intended, if there is any doubt. What is more, action itself has a conversational structure, for each act is a response to prior acts and expects other responses to it in turn. This makes sense only in a social context. Human life is essentially social, and human beings are in effect a part of each other. I am not myself alone, but other people are a part of my existence also.

Naturalism in philosophy and theology wants not to play the game of responsibility. It would like to be excused from giving reasons, excused from the ambiguity and anxiety of interpreting human actions. In naturalism, people would like to be excused from taking responsibility for their own actions. "It was nature in me that did it, not I myself." Nature may be the nature of psychology, or of astrology, of fortune or fate, or of evolution, cognitive science and artificial intelligence. There are doubtless other naturalistic models for human action. Naturalism would also prefer not to be seen not to play: people doing naturalism would like it to appear that the game of responsibility doesn't make sense or doesn't exist. For if the game can be seen, then they can be seen not to play, and that is too close to a visibly responsible choice.

I don't think that most naturalistic life orientations are conducted in the spirit of the irresponsible and reluctant tennis player that we began with, but the effect is the same. It is impossible to elicit serious acknowledgement of human freedom and human responsibility from people whose basic life orientation is naturalistic.

Chapter 6

Here's The Tell

6.1 Nature's Ways

How did it all get started? Where did people first start to think historically? That, as it turns out, is easier to answer if we first look at culture *before* historical thinking appeared. The aboriginal culture in every continent has been focused on nature. It was a naturalism, though a naturalism not entirely like the modern scientific naturalisms. Naturalism in religion sometimes has a "sacred," sometimes not. In its ancient and shamanistic varieties, it does. And in its Christian variety, it does also. There are modern non-Christian naturalistic religions that do have a sacred, of sorts: deep ecology, astrology, and the pagan revivals. But in the modern scientific variety of naturalism, people would like to exclude the sacred entirely. This is what used to go by the name of "scientific atheism." But the sacred to be excluded was a sacred derived from history and historical (i.e., Biblical) religion. In one Christian variety of naturalism, Biblical religion has been preserved, but it also has been forced to speak the language of scientific naturalism. That is the naturalistic theology with which we began.

The ancient naturalisms were different. Fortunately some still survive, today, in aboriginal cultures, and they have been studied by anthropologists. Aboriginal naturalism is a thing of great beauty. It is not an attempt to drive out all that is sacred, it has a sacred, but it locates the sacred in nature. In this sense, it is akin to modern religious naturalisms, for modern Christian naturalism insists on finding its (Biblical) sacred also present in nature on naturalistic terms. That, after all, was why we were looking for acts of God in quantum fluctuations when we began this book. What makes the aboriginal naturalistic religion naturalistic is its conception of nature. Its nature has more than you might think in common with modern scientific understanding of nature. For in both, nature is what is orderly. Order here means what is predictable, what is regular, what follows laws. "Nature has her ways"—and those ways are repeatable, predictable, lawful, orderly. History is disorderly, and history is not yet seen in the aboriginal cultures of the world.

Some things follow from this understanding of order in the world. Order has other meanings also, more general meanings. The orderly can merely mean what is under control, what is friendly to human beings, what is friendly to you and me. The state of the world need not be predictable or regular in order to be friendly. But being predictable and regular is one way to be friendly, if human beings can fit into that natural order. If order means being regular, anything that deviates from regular order is in some sense bad. It is chaos, because it is meaningless. Nature's ways are the only meaning there is here. It is dangerous, because the unpredictable is something you can't plan for. And what you can't plan for may kill you.

If the good is the orderly and regular, and the bad is what deviates from regular order, then fixing the bad means putting it back in order. One of the purposes of religion will always be to fix things that have gone wrong, to bring order back to life. This is almost definitional: whatever people do, at the highest level, to bring meaning back into their lives, is defined to be their religion. In naturalistic religion, where order is regularity, the rituals of religion are designed to bring all things back into that regular order. Cosmogony, in naturalistic religion, shows us the world at the beginning, when it was all in order. Religion is designed to restore that order. And so the New Year's festivals of the original religions everywhere are rituals that restore order.

One of the features of regular order, the order of natural laws, is that things are repeatable. This is the test of good science today, for a natural law has not been observed until other scientists can repeat your work in their laboratories. But natural order is repeatability at a deeper level. For in the life of the cosmos, if things do repeat themselves, in cycles, then they are orderly. These are called *cosmic* cycles. Cultures that think in terms of cosmic cycles usually have many levels of cycles, of which the shortest are familiar. The shortest cycle is, of course, just the day, the alternation of light and dark in a twenty-four hour period. The moon comes around once every twenty-eight or twenty-nine days. The sun moves through the sky once a year. The solar and lunar eclipse cycle was a lot harder to detect, and it is somewhat more subtle. (This pattern of eclipses is known as the "Saros" cycle.) When an eclipse threatens to take away one of the lights that people live by, it is a catastrophe of the first order. When it is hard to predict, the knowledge by which it can be predicted is that much greater an achievement. As it happens, eclipses fall in a pattern, and the eclipse pattern takes almost exactly 18 years. For modern astronomy, this is just a coincidence, but for the ancient world, it was one of the central meanings of life. The Saros cycle was known widely, but not everywhere. Even more subtle is the precession of the equinoxes. It was discovered in about 125 BCE by Hipparchus, a Greek astronomer, who deduced it from observations of surpassing difficulty. (A twenty-minute discrepancy in the timing of the winter solstice led to his discovery.) A short few years later, a new religion, Mithraism, was focused on precession, but it would take us too far afield to go into it here. The cycle of precession takes about 26,000 years. To discover it at all was a major achievement. Something that slow is subtle, something that large is important. You can see why people were impressed. The ability to discover order where before none was suspected was a major vindication for naturalistic religion.

It is important to notice that everything we call peculiarly historical would be viewed as disorder in a naturalistic culture. History is what is unpredictable, free. Whatever is intentional is free and so also not entirely predictable. Everything that we consider historical would have been considered part of disorder, and so part of the "bad" stuff of life, a good candidate for reduction to order. The social order in a nature religion is supposed to be like the natural order, indeed, *part* of the natural order. As such, it cannot be changed, and it is not something that human beings have made. What people have not made, they cannot take responsibility for.

Of such things as we have seen are cosmic cycles built; mythological imagination has had a lot to work with, and it has embroidered its material and enriched it fantastically. There is more than this in a life oriented to the orderly rhythms of nature. It is not just astronomical phenomena. The sky, the weather, waters, stones, human fertility, vegetable cycles, all the features of the biological world display regular patterns of one sort or another. And they all have a place in nature religions.

There are characteristic ways in which people relate to nature when nature is the locus of the sacred. It is human in any religion (not just nature religions) to set apart time to rest and focus on one's own relation to larger things. It is usually better to be alone, undistracted, so that you can concentrate. What follows, with abstinence from food, is sometimes ecstatic, a vision. Perhaps animals will come and speak to the seeker of visions. Perhaps he will be transported on a journey. Perhaps other natural phenomena will go out of their way to speak to him. People who could do this were called shamans in North Asia, but the phenomenon of seeking visions is universal. The term was borrowed by anthropologists as a name for the role in nature religions everywhere. The shaman is the "priest" of nature religions, for the shaman is the one who is in touch with the world of nature. He is the one for whom its invisible human significance is visible. He can see where ordinary people cannot. (And often the shaman was a she; it was by no means only a male thing.)

One last thing, and we are done. Nature religions in their original form treat the world as basically good. Human life is part of nature, and as such, it is good. Your job is to fit into nature naturally. This is what it means to "succeed" in life. Success means affirming the natural world as good and fitting into that good. That is why you could call this way of life a "world-affirming nature religion."

Nevertheless, this kind of religion finds it almost impossible to affirm as good things that it cannot understand in terms of nature. And so much of history remains unredeemed, written off as barren and evil.

6.2   Wetback Riff-Raffs

Once again, how did historical thinking get started? Where did people first make their religion historical? The simple answer has to be that historical thinking arose where there was first naturalistic thinking. And as it happened, it did, but it came about by a breach of order. Social order is supposed to be part of natural order, for nature religions.

We all know the story of the burning bush. What is not generally recognized is that in that story, Moses is a typical shaman, and he has a vision that is (almost) typical for a shaman. The shaman goes out alone into the wilderness, light on food, and soon a vision comes. Something marvelous in nature will happen, and the marvelous is not necessarily a violation of order for these people. The marvel will have human significance, and it will show the humans how to get back into harmony with nature. A burning bush surely qualifies as such a shaman's vision. So far, so good.

But Moses gets instructions to do a very un-shamanly thing. He is to lead a lot of people *out* of the social order of Egypt. Necessarily, since the social order is part of the natural order, he is to commit a major breach of the natural order. Shamans are supposed to restore order, not destroy it.

The background to this story is familiar enough. The "hebrews"— I put the word in quotes, because it has more meanings than just the proper name of a tribe—were peoples from southwest Asia (or northwest Arabia, take your pick) who were living in Egypt at the time. They were not particularly happy with their lot.

The word "hebrew" comes from a common word in the languages of that region, "hapiru." The "p" has been hardened into a "b", and the vowels have slipped around some, as vowels tend to do. What the word *means* is lower-class transient migrant laborer. Probably *not* ethnic Egyptian, though enough ethnic Egyptians left with the Hebrews in the Exodus. Migrant laborers come from all ethnic backgrounds,

and the dominant culture doesn't much care. They are all just resident
aliens. Useful when they are useful, a nuisance when they are not.
Their leaving is not noted in any Egyptian records.

Now these people were of a transient background, migrants, no-
mads, used to desert life. Going out into the desert to worship one of
the local volcano and earthquake deities would be normal enough for
them. The Egyptians apparently thought they just wanted to quit work
early, and forbade the excursion. The rest of the story is also familiar
enough. Some of us have read it, some of us have seen Charlton Hes-
ton playing the role of Moses in the movies. Moses and Aaron have a
bad argument with Pharaoh, and they all leave Egypt in a trip marked
by anomalous weather, wind, and sea conditions. They escape to the
east, into the Sinai desert. There the story gets harder to follow, and
not quite so dramatic. They run out of food, the locals are not friendly,
and then they wait at the bottom of a volcano while Moses goes up
on the mountain and gets the Ten Commandments. The trip on into
the promised land is not so dramatic, and does not lend itself to easy
memory.

There are major human consequences for this excursion, and they
tend to be missed in all the eye-catching special effects. One clue
that is easily overlooked is a scant sentence, hardly a phrase: "they
were joined by a mixed multitude" (Exodus 12.38). Numbers 11.4
repeats the same thing. The Revised Standard Version has "a mixed
multitude went with them," and the Jerusalem Bible has "people of
various sorts joined them in great numbers." (I am relying here on
biblical scholarship that would take far too long to summarize, but
these things are commonly accepted among scholars today.) In fact,
though the text makes it appear that they were all descendents of one
patriarch, Jacob and his twelve sons, the people who left Egypt were
probably an ethnic mix. There were a lot of tribes who had come
together in Egypt, they were all suffering under a government they did
not particularly like, and it is not surprising that they all left together.
They may even not all have come out of Egypt; different parts of the
story may have been contributed by different tribes who joined them
later. And some who came with them were Egyptians; "Moses" is an

Egyptian name, and some of the characters later on in the story also have Egyptian names.

In a happy society with a world-affirming nature religion, there is a place for everybody, and it appears that everybody gets taken care of. It looks that way because the horizon is so constricted. Ethnic others are invisible. In times of scarcity, nature religion is hard-put to produce happiness. Later on, when you try to build an empire, not everybody gets well taken care of. Some are slaves or just lower classes, left out when it comes time for the good things in life. Building an empire on the basis of a nature-religion is what the Egyptians did; the Pharaoh was high priest and a god as well as the earthly ruler. He was the symbol of natural order and social order at the same time. Those who were left out, at the bottom, may be excused if they were not impressed.

Leaving such a society would have been understandable. But there is nothing in a nature religion that can hold diverse peoples together. For the ways of nature tend to keep different tribes apart. They have different gods, and their different gods often war with each other, just as the tribes themselves warred with each other. The "natural" thing would have been for them to split up once they were free of Egypt, and go their separate ways. They did not.

Perhaps they were afraid, out in the desert; perhaps they were kept together because they needed each other in the face of enemies in the desert. Who knows all the reasons. But stay together they did, and so they were doubly in violation of the ways of nature. Once for leaving the social order that was the perfection of natural order, and once for violating tribal ways. There is more, as we shall see.

If they were to stay together, they needed some basis for staying together, and that would require something new, since nature religion doesn't provide any such basis. Nature religion is what they had to work with, and they improvised, modifying it so that it could keep them together. And so Moses's original shaman's vision, the one in which he saw the burning bush, becomes a job interview with the local volcano deity, but that deity has been given a new job. That deity is to lead them out of nature and into history. They do not know that yet, and they are none too sure they really want to go. Nature, the predictable and orderly, is a source of comfort, and more to the point, a source of food. They complain. "Were there not graves enough in Egypt, that you had to bring us out here to die?" There is no water one day. There is no food the next. Then the locals are out to kill them.

Since what it means to live in history is not at all clear to them, they are anxious at a deeper level than just food and enemies. Where nature is predictable, history is the unpredictable. Where nature is orderly, history is disorderly. Where nature can be relied upon, in history, it is very much like being out in the desert. You do not know where your next meal is coming from.

Yet they kept one thing from nature religion at its best. Nature religion at least tries to be world-affirming. And so the first historical religion was also world-affirming. World-affirming historical religion means to say that human life is essentially historical, and as such, is good. Two things come with this. First, we cannot understand human lives except with the openness of narrative that we have seen already in the example of our teen-age friend who went cruising. Naturalistic descriptions can't explain the things that matter most to us. And second, it is not always easy to affirm human life—whether it is part of nature *or* history. History does not make it any easier. If anything, history makes it harder. Unpacking the world-*affirming* part of world-affirming historical religion will occupy us for the rest of this book.

6.3   I Be First Tracker

Some kind of agreement was needed to stay together. The agreement is more than just saying "Let's stick together and help each other out," but that's the general idea for at least part of it. If doing this is what it's really all about for human life, if this is what ultimate reality really is, then this is not *just* something that human beings have cooked up together. If you can tolerate a fifty-dollar word, *historicality*, being made of history, is something that is imposed on human life, not created by human beings. You can acknowledge it or not, but it is there regardless. As a matter of faith, historicality brings good, life more abundantly. This is the world-affirming part, and it was a necessary part of the agreement in the desert. Without it, why bother? If the desert would eat them up in the end, why affirm human life in this world?

They did make it, they did survive, and they did so not entirely through their own efforts. Things came together. The first, of course, was the anomalous weather and the dry land in the middle of the Sea of Reeds. Spectacular enough, visual and memorable enough. When it looked like their only choice was between drowning and being slaughtered, the sea opened up before them and let them through—and then swallowed up their pursuers. This is not the sort of thing that you forget. Nor do you forget what it meant for you: when all was darkest, you were provided for. It was a kind of doorway, from nature into history, though that became clear only long, long afterward. As I have said before, what something is can be changed after the fact, by changing the narrative it fits into. The Exodus, for example. It only became a doorway into history later, when these peoples had gotten used to history, and to affirming life in history in spite of its pains. But in hindsight, it was clearly the turning point.

Now we have already seen the difference between people living in nature and people living in history, in *Thunderdome*. The people of Bartertown were doing their best to live in a world of nature; certainly they had no hopes for history other than something like the history of empire-building. The Tribe at the Oasis in the desert, by contrast, had a real history, and they had real hope for history. They told their story repeatedly to make sure they would not forget it. The "Tell," they called it. Well, here's The Tell, the *original* Tell. It's very short. I have put it into modern language so you can see what it really felt like:

> My father was a wandering Aramaean, few in number, and he went down from Syria into Egypt, to the Big City. And there he became a great nation, with lots of people. And then the local management changed. The new management was not particularly friendly, and treated us harshly. So we complained, to El Jefe, the Boss, our fa-

thers' Boss, and he heard our complaining, and brought us with a mighty hand and arm outstretched, on wings of eagles, out of the frying pan, through the fire, into this, the promised land. (With apologies to Deuteronomy 26.5–9)

This was said later, when they were in the promised land. Among other occasions, it was recited at the harvest festivals, so that they should not turn back to nature, but remember their history, and be grateful. In one particularly bad episode, centuries later, when things were going badly, Amos the prophet begins with indictments of all the tinpot kingdoms in the area. They were all mistreating each other. After Damascus, Gaza, Tyre, Edom, Ammon, Moab, and Judah, he comes to little Israel. The indictment starts out just like the others, but it is twice as long. The second half is different. The Boss says,

And Oh, *by the way*—I'm the one who brought you out of Egypt! I'm the one who brought you into this land! But you forgot. Then you became ungrateful. Ungrateful, you were nasty to your neighbors. If you had studied history, you might have passed instead of flunked. Then you would have been grateful, and if you had been grateful, you would have been nice to your neighbors. (With apologies to Amos 2.6–16.)

Remember our escapees from Egypt, trying to stick together and help each other out? A lot grew out of that experience.

This short historical creed as it has been called, the Original Tell, has shaped a lot more than just the few verses on either side of it in Deuteronomy. What with all the strange weather, the edible dust in the desert in place of the leeks and onions and garlic of Egypt, you might miss it. But it shapes the entire narrative, and it gets repeated, with more or less the same parts and variations only in style, until fairly late in the history of the texts. For example, not until Nehemiah, late after the return from the Babylonian Exile, is the bit about the Law, the Ten Commandments, inserted into the story. I am following Gerhard Von Rad's famous essay, "The Problem of the Hexateuch," fairly closely here (Von Rad, 1984). The Tell gets repeated in Deuteronomy 6.20–24, Joshua 24.2–13, Psalms 105, 106, and 136, among other places. And of course, it shapes the narrative of the Exodus itself.

Some people have suggested than Von Rad, a Christian scholar, had less than charitable intentions toward Rabbinic Judaism, and intended to make something of the fact that the Sinai and Law tradition seems to have been originally independent and was joined to the Exodus tradition only later. Perhaps. I don't know Von Rad's motives, but I want no part of anything anti-Jewish. And in any case, the Law is essential, as we shall see in the next section. It is essential for Christian heirs of the Exodus just as much as it is for Jewish heirs today, if not entirely in the same way. The point here is simply to recognize this short historical creed as the core and shape of a much larger narrative.

One could ask, what were these riff-raffs, these hapiru, *doing* when they got out of Egypt? This question is very much like the question of what our teen-age friend was doing on that August Friday evening. The events could be fitted into many narratives, in both cases. Which is the one that matters? For you?

From the point of view of weather-science, these people were just out in a storm without any raincoats. The crossing was not at the Red Sea, but at a long narrow inlet from it, the Sea of Reeds. And the parting of the Sea of Reeds has been simulated on a computer; it is unusual, but in no sense is it a "violation of natural laws." Those interested may consult Nof and Paldor (1992). Doron Nof and Nathan Paldor found a hideously nonlinear differential equation that describes pretty much what is reported in Exodus. Exquisitely hideous, for those who like such equations. But a differential equation just the same, one telling what happens when the wind blows long enough to expose a sand-bar in a shallow inlet with a bottom that slopes uniformly out to sea.

Remember the problem with which we began, long ago? Which fluctuations are acts of God, which ones are just random fluctuations of the kind that physics knows? Cause laundering will have a fairly easy time making this look like an Act of God that can be known *in the language of physics*. For there are so many places to hide unaccountable causes in the fluctuations that build up into global weather patterns. Even so, if we do that, the physicists will grumble. (I know; I am a physicist, and I would grumble.) It is easier to take our model from the cruising teen-ager and see if there are not more possible narratives that we can fit these events into. When we see how many different narratives the parting of the Sea of Reeds can be fitted into if it is to be considered an act at all, it becomes odd to single out a naturalistic explanation and then bend that explanation to make it look like the supernatural.

From the point of view of sociology, of course, these peoples came and went. Hostages, prisoners of war, even merchants, once in Egypt, their circumstances did not improve. From time to time, such people left.

From the point of view of the Egyptians, these people might as well not have existed. There is no record of them at all.

From the point of view of history of ideas and history of technology, two things are of importance. With spreading metal technology, it was possible to build empires that had a global vision. This makes it possible to see far enough, to have broad enough cultural horizons, so that history becomes conceivable. The other prerequisite is writing. For without writing, it's not possible to remember enough details to have a history, to have a narrative that you can go back over and question. Once these requirements are in place, the rest is not surprising. Sooner or later, somewhere, sometime, someone will turn world-affirming nature religion into world-affirming historical religion. That it happened here is just an accident, not something that needs an explanation.

Christians like to think that the real change in religion came only much later, in the time of Jesus. But the first century, time of change though it was, produced nothing like the radical change that came at the Exodus. The real watershed in the history of religions is at the Exodus, not in the disasters of the first century. Both Christianity and Rabbinic Judaism were groups seeking a way to continue the inheritance from the Judaism of the Second Temple, the temple that the Romans destroyed. (The temple that the Romans destroyed in 70 CE was the second; the first was destroyed by the Babylonians in 586

BCE.) The changes of the first century were just changes from one kind of historical religion to another. The change at the Exodus was a change from nature religion to something radically different.

From another point of view in the history of religions, this was a natural development of Canaanite religion. The peoples who came into Canaan were somewhat diverse, and they borrowed ideas and texts from each other liberally. Israelite religion was no exception. For only one example, Psalm 29, the hymn to God as Lord of the Storm, is largely plagiarized from an Ugaritic hymn to Baal, lord of the storm; only the name of the deity has been changed. The creation stories in Genesis have parallels, in part, in other ancient near eastern documents. Things become a little clearer in the time of David and Solomon. The history before that time is not easy to pin down. The Exodus is a cycle of traditions that were first put in stable written form in the early years of the Monarchy, though some texts were much older (the Song of the Sea, in Exodus 15, for one example).

From within the house of Israel, there are more possibilities still. The stories serve the needs of later tribal and priestly clans. Moses and Aaron represent different factions in the kingdoms of Israel and Judah. Indeed, many actors in the Exodus story foreshadow later actors during the Monarchy. So much so that the earlier story has been seriously shaped by the later history. For those who want to know more, Richard Elliott Friedman's *Who Wrote the Bible?* (1989) is an excellent introduction.

What does it all mean if today you want to affirm human life in history? What does it mean if you want to be like these people who stumbled from nature into history, thirty-odd centuries ago? Well, for starters, you identify with them. With a little further digging, you identify with their literary executors, the later writers who told their story for their own later purposes. This not a trivial undertaking, for most of the actors in the story did some questionable things. Even Moses didn't get to go into the promised land. David was a first-class power politician, and Solomon was a despot. His son was just plain stupid, as the reader may be appalled or entertained to discover in 1 Kings.

But several features of affirming life in history should stand out. The human experience of doing it today means, to be sure, that history itself is open to some revision, open to responsible debate about what was happening. (This we called the activity of responsibility a few sections ago.) We see this openness of history because we know that the events can be fitted into multiple narratives. There are many ways to make sense of the events, and indeed, many ways to decide what the events were, even after you know what the physical motions were. Merely knowing the physical motions of the past in history doesn't help you much when you want to know the significance of the *actions*. And what counts as an action in history (as opposed to nature) means that the historian has made a selection, what counts as part of the action, what does not. Did we have the exodus of a *group* out of Egypt, or only a lot of individuals out in a windstorm? Neither physics nor any other natural science can tell us that.

There is something even more striking about the experience of affirming human life in history as good. It shows itself when things don't seem to be going so well. The good in life comes to you when you are not in control. When you could not just make it happen, it happens to you. The good in life comes to you as a gift. But to say that is to speak in metaphors, analogies, for there is no giver within history, within the world. This is certainly not to speak any kind of naturalistic language. These analogies, however, are the stuff of history, what history is like from the inside. It would be virtually impossible to explain what history is like from the inside without such language. We shall come to it again.

6.4   Seven Lessons

Remember our escaped riff-raffs, fresh out of Egypt, looking for a way to stay together? "Before Sinai there had been high gods, nature gods, ancestral gods, and gods of the polis, but there had never been a high God of escaped slaves and declassed fugitives." (Rubenstein, 1992, p. 143.) This would be a different kind of deity.

Our escapees learned from their experience, and learned a lot, which might surprise you, since they complained so much. Those riff-raffs learned some seven lessons as they became one people. (I found seven, but there may be more.) Let me introduce them briefly and then make some comments on them.

(1) They had no use for governments that arrogated to themselves divine power. For these people, no human institutions are sacred. This much is clear from their mistreatment at the hands of the Egyptian sacral kingship. Here is the root of civil and political freedom, for the move to desacralize human institutions at the same time was a move to hold governments responsible.

(2) They could not become one people if they were to retain their previous ethnic- and nature-based identities. The companion principle to the desacralizing of governments was a community of moral obligation which was in principle open to all and from which none could be excluded who wished to join. This was a necessity if they were to become one people. This is familiar in the commandment to love one's neighbor as another like oneself. The situation out of which this arises, ethnic plurality, did not become clear until biblical scholarship of the last century or so pieced it out of scattered hints in the texts. The unity that was forged out of this plurality was in fact a pluralistic unity.

(3) If these peoples were to become one, they would have to surrender or at least relativize everything that separated them. The deities of nature lose their ultimate status at this point. To consummate such a move to history, they had to desacralize nature itself. What is kept from the world-affirming nature religions is the affirmation of this world, and of nature in it, even when nature is no longer sacred.

(4) Human life necessarily has some focus of loyalty, confidence, and meaning (at least it does if it is coherent), and that focus had to be placed outside of the forces and phenomena of nature and beyond human institutions: in something transcendent. I find the Shema implicitly present at this point, the command in Deuteronomy, "Hear, O Israel, the Lord is our God, the Lord alone." The first three commandments of the Decalog grow out of this. The term that I invoke at this point, "transcendence," is of recent coinage (Placher, 1996), but the

roots of the concept in human practices can be confidently located here in the Exodus and the texts that have come down to us from it.

(5) The believer is to welcome the transcendent holy into the world, rather than seeking escape to it from the world. (This is a radical difference from something that only came later, and was not world-affirming at all. That religion is known in the West as Gnosticism, and it is not part of our story.) This lesson is the point at which the world is affirmed in all its pains as good. The world in its pains is then something to be consummated and perfected (the Hebrew word for this is *tikkun*), not something to be escaped from or trashed or merely used.

(6) A project such as this one must in order to work have some kind of behavioral standards which inculcate these loyalties. These standards will be inculturated somewhat differently in different times and places. As the tradition has it, these standards were the Law given at Sinai. The age of that tradition is not entirely clear. In any case, the Law has been greatly developed, locally adapted, and amended since its origins.

(7) Last, but not least, there was to be continuing attention to past history in order to keep this confidence for future history in perspective, with its hazards, obligations, and promises. Other items could be added, but I think these are among the most important. The order among them is to some extent arbitrary.

Look at the inter-relationships between these seven features of the Exodus.

I have put first the relativizing of human governments and institutions because it grows most directly out of the Hebrews' experience of oppression at the hands of a government that absolutized itself. As the concepts grew, this one came to be dependent on the fourth, the turn to a transcendent Other: if human institutions are to be relativized, then they are made relative *to* something else. It was the prohibition on locating that Other within the world of nature or human institutions that lies at the root of the later understanding of transcendence, though that understanding appears at the start in the prohibition of visual images.

The transcendent reality is then to be loved. "Love" is doubtless too weak a word for the human attitude toward a reality that is mysterious, both attractive and awesome, and in its awesomeness, a little terrifying. One is dependent before this Reality, not a peer to it. But the Shema has "love," and sacred fear has to be understood as part of that love. This ultimate reality is to be loved even when it brings disappointments. This religion will not be entirely easy.

It took a long time for the desacralizing of human governments to develop into the kind of liberty that the modern world knows, or even for the structured liberties that the medieval polities knew. Nevertheless, the root is here. The modern sense of vigilance for liberty against governments that arrogate to themselves absolute power comes from the departure from Egyptian sacral kingship. As history testifies, the Egyptian arrangements were common, and modern returns to absolute government have happened all too often, in every age since.

The move to desacralize nature along with human institutions bears some comment. It is easy to overlook the degree to which nature, ethnicity, and human institutions were all of a piece in the world-view of the second millennium BCE. Then, one could not disestablish one without disestablishing all three. Yet even in the modern world, where they can be separated, it is not really possible to center the focus of human loyalty in nature if it is also to be located as something manifest in history. Nature does not become less awesome or less beautiful when it becomes less sacred. The root question here is whether human beings will understand themselves in terms of nature or history. The challenge to human self-understanding, both as offer of opportunity, and as critique and exposure, potential reproach, comes at the point where human actions are to be characterized. And the best that nature can do by way of understanding human action is a pathetic shadow of what history does.

Though the sacred is to be met "in" history, that does not mean that the sacred is an actor in history in the same sense that other actors are. The sacred is manifest in history in ways that it is not in nature. But for purposes of external history, it rules no empires, passes no laws, collects no taxes, wars no wars, and so on. Human beings do all these things. To be sure, some, who stood in the Exodus tradition, spoke of their God being also their king, as if the sacred *could* indeed rule, legislate, tax, war, and so on. The Bible has quite enough of such language. Yet standing in the present, seeing what we can see, with the distinctions that we can make, we have to say that, no, the "divine" does not act in history—in anything like the may that ordinary mortals do, whether lowly or high-born. That does not rule out *other* ways in which transcendence could show itself in history, and so "act." I put "divine" and "act" in scare-quotes because it is still not very clear how they might work in a historical religion.

We distinguished above between the transcendent, the immanent, and the intramundane. History in some ways parallels nature at this point. For history as merely the intramundane, what we later called "external" history, no more has room for God as an explanation than does nature. Yet transcendence has an immanent presence, a presence in history that does not disturb or displace any intramundane actors. That presence shows itself where human beings, in making sense of their own experience, naturally borrow the language of human action and interpersonal experience, to make sense of their experience of life as a whole, of the cosmos as a whole, of ultimate reality.

God is no more an intramundane historical actor than he is an intramundane natural cause. That is to say, God is ruled out as an explanation in "external" history, the historical narratives in which the narrator is not asking about his own responsibility or the consequences for his own life. In "internal" history, where the lives of the narrator and his community are at stake, what best brings to language the human experience of history is (or at least, was) the language of human relationships, borrowed by analogy and transferred for use in making sense of the cosmos.

One may protest at this point, and protest fairly, that such a move is "subjective." All analogies are. We see again the issue with which we began, a desire to be responsible (which "objectivity" was supposed to supply), and a desire to avoid being left holding the bag (which subjectivity supposedly implied). Responsibility is both sought and feared.

Let me note last something we shall meet again, the fifth lesson, that transcendence is to be welcomed into the world. This is because the world is good, and human life in the world is affirmed as good. The alternative is to locate transcendence utterly outside the world, because the world is bad and defective. That alternative is one that we do not consider in this book; it is called gnosticism, and it is not part of our story. The choice that we are interested in, to affirm human life in a world that has so much pain in it, will be a lot of work. It is easier in a superficial sense not to affirm the world and life in it. We shall explore only the affirmative side of that choice, in order to keep this book within manageable limits and to stay close to the central focus on the difference between history and nature. But it is only fair to note that it is not necessary to affirm human life in this world, either as nature or as history. Other possibilities do exist.

6.5 $\pi = 4$

One could complain, with some justice, that all this business about a historical religion is made up, a human artifact. Of course, the ancient nature religions were then all made up, too, also human artifacts. To those who are innocent of the history of science, modern science can have the appearance of *not* being a human artifact. Historians know better. Science developed when and where it did for contingent cultural reasons, and particular theoretical moves in the sciences have equally human reasons behind them. Yet the objection persists. Science is about nature, and nature is just there, it does not have the openness of characterization that human actions in history do. Perhaps. I would like to deal with history, in any case, where human responsibility is undeniable.

The human artifact that is most central and most questionable is the one in which human life in history is *affirmed*, taken as good, in spite of its pains. We shall be unpacking this idea for some time. Without it, historical religion of the biblical variety would be pointless. One would be left only with other choices—world-affirming nature religions, ancient or modern, world-rejecting religions, or religions that live in history but see no transcendent, and affirm only parts of human life in history.

It seems outrageous to stand in history, in full view of its pains, and then affirm that human life in history. The next few sections will be about what you have to *do* to live that affirmation. This one is about what it means to make this affirmation of the cosmos.

There is a technical term in the business for this sort of affirmation. It is called a "covenant." A covenant is not quite the same thing as a contract, but they are similar. Two parties make an agreement. In a contract, the obligations of each party are spelled out and *limited*. The parties to a contract are in some sense symmetrical. In a covenant, the two parties are not of equal stature, the relationship is not symmetrical, and the obligations are not limited. One party, the party of lesser stature, has open-ended obligations. The covenant, once voluntarily entered into, cannot be renounced.

The *form* for the first covenants was borrowed from local diplomatic treaties, and we shall come to it momentarily. The modern ear, I think, is inclined to reject the whole idea as make-believe, make-believe that the cosmos will be good to us, when in fact the cosmos doesn't know or care about us. But the covenanters knew this, and what they intended and represented as the Other Party is not the cosmos taken as a whole, nor anything within the cosmos, but something transcendent. It was not supernatural, even though the language they used is easy to mistake for talk about a supernatural. (We have already deflated the supernatural as just an extension of the natural by other means.) Transcendence is hard to articulate, except in analogies, and then the analogies are always open to misuse. The fact that the literary genre chosen to express this new idea was that of a treaty between lord and vassal expresses in its own second-millennium BCE way a sense that one is dealing with transcendence, not with intramundane actors or with nature.

That literary genre was the form of what are called "Hittite suzerainty treaties," the treaties that Hittite emperors imposed on conquered cities. The Hittites were a people now long lost save for a few stones as remnants, probably of Indo-European origin, living in Anatolia, that is to say in what is now central and eastern Turkey. Their reach extended well down into Syria, Palestine, and parts of Mesopotamia. The Hittite Empire lasted from around 1650 BCE until around 1200 BCE.

When a Hittite king or emperor conquered and subdued another city, the ruler of that city became a vassal to the Hittite emperor by a treaty that is known as a "suzerainty" treaty, because the emperor was declared to be suzerain or lord, and the vassal undertook the appropriate obligations to the superior power. Such a treaty characteristically had six parts, though not all parts are present in all examples. A few Hittite suzerainty treaties in translation have been posted on the Net, and many more are available in print.

The parts are (1) the identity of the suzerain, (2) the past benefits he has conferred on the vassal, (3) the obligations imposed on the vassal, (4) rewards and penalties for keeping or breaking the covenant, (5) gods invoked as witnesses, and (6) provision for regular public reading of the document. The second and sixth correspond to the seventh lesson of the Exodus, the injunction to remember and to study history. This language was borrowed and used often in the texts we have in the Bible. In effect, the human experience of political relations in the imperial ancient near east was borrowed and used to make sense of human life as a whole, of the cosmos as a whole. This borrowing all by itself is a human act for which people can (and should) take responsibility. It was not particularly visible then *as* a human act; the analogies just came instinctively. Today, when analogy is more visible and much disputed, it entails a responsibility that could not have been seen then.

Perhaps the most problematic part of the suzerainty treaty pattern is its second part, the rehearsal of past benefits and promise of future benefits. For if we limit ourselves to nature or to external history, there are no actors that could give the kind of benefits intended, and the goods of the past were not the result of "acts" at all. But this covenant language is part of the language of internal history; it tells what it means to be a part of this covenant community. This part of the covenant is a promise, a promise of blessing, a promise of life more abundantly. It is a promise put in the mouth of the divine partner by the human authors of the documents, the human actors who borrowed local diplomatic texts to make sense of their lives and the cosmos as a whole. And this promise is one conceived in full view of the ample pains of life.

What may come as a surprise is that there are *many* covenants in the Bible, not just one. To take only a few, there are no less than three made with Abraham. In the first, Genesis 12, Abraham has no obligations whatsoever. God promises him lots of children (no small promise in those days), and says that he will be a blessing to all peoples. If he has any obligation at all, that is it. In Genesis 15 and Genesis 17, there are variations on this covenant, and Abraham does have obligations here (circumcision, in chapter 17). In the Exodus, there are at least two sets of ten commandments (Exodus 20 and 34), and they are not really the same. Variations and extensions and repetitions occur all the way through Deuteronomy. There is an entirely new covenant with the Monarchy, the kingdom of David. Its story is told in the books of Samuel. 2 Samuel 7 is the central text, Nathan's prophecy to David. The House of David will apparently rule over the Israelites in perpetuity. Yet that promise is broken two short generations later—Solomon's son Rehoboam is so stupid that the ten northern tribes secede and become the kingdom of Israel, leaving little Judah to the heirs of David. And both kingdoms come to an end a few centuries later, Israel to the Assyrians in 722, and Judah to the Babylonians in 586 BCE. Psalm 89 records the sense of betrayal on the part of the Israelites. You promised! How could you do such a thing to us?!

So it is easy to see the problem. Human beings concoct the hair-brained notion that ultimate reality will deliver some schedule of goods and blessings, and then things turn out about as we would expect from our knowledge of intramundane causes and actors. The "promised" blessings are transient. Human faithlessness does not surprise us, but divine faithlessness leaves us feeling betrayed. How much easier to forget about transcendence, not to affirm human life in this world unconditionally, and instead just work with intramundane causes and actors, trying to get the best deal we can negotiate, and let our neighbors fend for themselves as best they can.

There is a story, so often told and so little documented that it is now more legend than history, that early in the nineteenth century, one house in each of two state legislatures in what was then the Wild West (Tennessee and Indiana) each set the value of π to a convenient integer. I forget whether they chose 3 or 4. This has been the occasion of much ridicule. But how much different is it with a covenant?

Perhaps the way to say it is that the human partner in the covenant declares the terms of the covenant, but the transcendent partner, if we may speak of ultimate reality that way, disposes of how things actually turn out. We declare, God interprets. You *can* set π to 4, but you will of course find that reality has its own interpretation of your covenant, an interpretation not necessarily at all like yours. Hence the original covenanters' sense, back at the end of the second millennium BCE, that they were dealing with a "higher power."

They took the experience of being the weaker party, subject to the Hittites, and used that experience (and its language) to make sense of their relationship to—to what? Life as a whole? Ultimate reality? The Way Things Are? What we are grasping for (and gasping for) has no name. To give it a name courts the danger that it will then become confused with just one more phenomenon in nature or actor in history. And so in Moses' job interview in Exodus 3, Moses asks, "Who *are* you?," and gets only this non-answer: "I shall be with you as who I am shall I be with you" (Murray, 1964, pp. 5–12).

It is clear from casual knowledge of causes and actors within the world that affirming human life in this world simply in terms of intramundane factors will not work. The intramundane either doesn't care (nature) or is capricious and frequently malicious (history). It was because they knew all too well how much hurt causes and actors *within* the world can inflict that these people groped for a way to affirm life in terms of something radically *beyond* the world. That beyond, that transcendent, is always elusive. It is immanently present in the world, but is never one cause beside other physical causes, never one actor in history beside others. It is spoken of only by analogy.

Those analogies give voice to what a wise old woman in Simi Valley once said to me: So few people in this world ask for what they want, that those who do ask sometimes actually get it. But it's not a bad idea to think carefully about what one wants.

Chapter 7

How Much Does It Cost?

7.1 But History Hurts

We have seen already that where nature is orderly and predictable, history is disorderly and unpredictable. Nature religions reject the disorderly as evil, as a disruption and violation of the harmony of nature. Historical religion notices that much of human life is disorderly. Indeed, much of it cannot be understood at all in terms of the regular and lawful order of nature. The religion that we have seen in the Exodus was an attempt to make sense of life in some way other than in terms of the order, rhythms, and harmony of nature.

There is another problem here, besides just the question of natural order. The question about different kinds of explanation in nature and history is a rather theoretical question. More obvious is something simpler: The naturalistic religions rejected what people later came to know as history because history hurts. History is terror, history means cosmic catastrophe, military disaster, social injustice, personal misfortune. If nature is taken as the model for human affairs, things can make sense because they can be fitted into patterns. Pain that makes sense does not hurt a tenth as much as pain that is absurd. Without the comforts of a naturalistic cosmos, man stands alone before chaos, alone in the turbulence of history. If nature is not the model for human affairs, some other strategy must make sense of the pains of life.

Historical religion does make sense of the pains of life, contingent though they are. It interprets them on the analogy of the contingent will and intentions of a benevolent God. It is not simply that the pains are imposed by the will of God, but that somehow, within the larger intentions of the deity, the pains bear a blessing of some sort. Often the blessing is not seen but only trusted until it can be seen.

There are at least three different sorts of pain in life, and a characteristic way of handling each one. You can be frustrated in some attempted action, prevented from doing what you would like to, or find yourself with no happy or easy course of action at all. Let us call this kind of disappointment *limitation*, because in it one is faced with limitations on action. The next is a collection that may seem miscellaneous, but which has a common theme nonetheless. Another person can be abandoned, left alone, without company or solace; or without food or means of sustenance, in poverty; or sick and diseased; or barren, without children. Let us call this kind of disappointment *need*, for in it, the other person is in need, and needs your help. The last kind of disappointment might have escaped notice. It happens when you are caught red-handed, when other people can see what you really are like (instead of what you pretend to be). Call it *exposure*. In a more traditional order, these pains get listed as exposure, limitation, and need. They are an ancient series, but it was Edward Hobbs who first saw them *as* a series (1970).

There is a certain kind of symmetry, if one looks at these disappointments in the prototypical situation of encounter with *another* person. In exposure, one is exposed *to* another person; exposure doesn't make sense otherwise. As a child, the first experience of limitation occurs in the parent's will that the child do some things and not do other things. It is the encounter with another person's need that completes the series. The disappointment comes because the other person's need is a demand on my time, efforts, and resources when I would rather have kept them for myself. Even at the simplest level, I have to acknowledge a common humanity with the other who suffers, and that I would rather not do.

In brief, the positive response to each of these is very simple. One responds to exposure with acknowledgment and then amendment of life. One responds to limitation with innovation and gratitude, and to others' need with help as appropriate.

This series, exposure, limitation, and need, is characteristically Christian rather than Jewish. (There is more about it in *Unwelcome Good News*, yet to come.) Nevertheless, even though Judaism does not *organize* the disappointments in this tripartite series, it does respond positively in more or less the same ways that Christianity does. We do not see these themes *as a series* in the Common Documents or the Talmud in quite the way that they appear in the New Testament and Christian literature, but examples of each one appear in the Common Documents and the Talmuds nonetheless.

In some ways, need was the first to appear, in the Exodus, in the mutual need of the escapees from Egypt, an ethnically diverse lot of peoples. Nature as model for human affairs would have set them against each other rather than allowed them to help each other. They banded together and affirmed first of all their mutual obligation to each other in need. This was the second lesson of the Exodus in the list of seven that I found above. Again and again, the command to help the other in need appears. Deuteronomy is not the first nor the last voice on behalf of the needy, but it may be the clearest.

The event of exposure is classic in the prophets. It appears at its most excruciating in the encounter between David and Nathan after David has arranged the death of Uriah and taken Uriah's wife Bathsheba.

Limitation appears usually mixed with exposure, in the sense that some exposure is implicit in the limitation. Being conquered by the Assyrians and then Babylonians was limitation in the extreme. That the limitation should come as predicted was certainly heard by the prophets' audiences. That it could bring blessing made no sense. The blessing came usually in the form of challenge to repentance. This is turned around in the New Testament, where repentance and forgiveness of sins are often the prolog in each of the healing stories. The healing stories are about disability, or in other words, limitation.

Traditionally, in Christian circles, blessing in exposure is the work of God the Son, present in history in Jesus. This is redemption from sin, for what exposure exposes is usually sin. Limitation is the work of God the Father, the creator who imposes the limitations, which are also opportunities and blessings. Need is encountered in God the Holy Spirit, who brings sustenance of all kinds. The Rabbis were never very impressed with this organization, and even less convinced by its association with the disreputable Jesus crowd. Nevertheless, when push comes to shove, they do more or less the same things as Christians do: exposure is met with repentance, limitation with creativity, and need with open eyes, open hands, open heart. Even if it has nothing to do with Jesus. *Tikkun* is the Hebrew term for the repair of the pains of life, and exploring it would, if we had time, give us an authentically Jewish version of these things. Since the problem of this book is about the relations between history and nature, and since it has been a problem more for Christians than for Jews, and since I know more about Christianity than about Rabbinic Judaism, I beg to be allowed to focus on the Christian side of the House of the Exodus, and merely record my affection and esteem and respect for the other Exodus tradition. You Jews have fewer problems than we Christians do.

If one is to affirm human life in history, open-eyed, in full view of its pains, one must deal with exposure, limitation, and need. Are they to be avoided? Are they barren? Do they bring any good? Does the truth do you any good when the truth hurts? The answer, when I ask this question of students (captives that they are) is invariably in the affirmative, but hesitant, because they know that the hurt can be very real. The question hardly gets seen, much less asked, in face of limitation and need, though I think people do respond in the affirmative in practice, and people certainly admire others for doing so. If exposure, limitation, and need are barren, avoiding them is the right thing to do. Not to avoid them would be foolish. If exposure, limitation, and need bring blessing, then to avoid them is also to evade them. More than this, if all of life is good, then to reject its painful parts as barren is to make a big mistake. One wrongs not just oneself, but also other people, since they are often the victims of such a mistake.

7.2 Happy Easter

There are thirteen identified people healed in the Gospel of Mark. They come in a series, starting with small body parts (here a hand, there a leg), and progress to larger and larger things, culminating in whole-body healings. The healings are of two sorts, and most are marked with words that mean *cleanse* or *raise*. Interspersed among them are the feedings, one with seven loaves, one with five loaves. There is a thirteenth loaf a little too casually noted in story after the second feeding, when Jesus is in the boat with the disciples in a storm. Thirteen healings, some by cleansing, some by raising. Thirteen loaves.

After this series comes the cleansing of the Temple, the feeding of the disciples at the Last Supper, and the raising of Jesus, the Resurrection. There is a message here. Edward Hobbs noticed the series, and noticed that the sequence of "miracles" builds up to a climax. The little ones prepare you for the bigger ones, and the whole series prepares you for the three at the end.

The list:

The first five:
1.21 a demoniac
1.29 Simon's mother-in-law
1.40 a leper
2.1 a paralytic, lowered through the roof by his friends
3.1 the man with the withered hand

The second five, with feedings interspersed:
5.1 the Gerasene demoniac
5.21 Jairus' daughter
5.25 the woman with a hemorrhage
6.30 (five loaves)
7.24 the Syro-phoenician woman's daughter
7.31 the deaf-mute
8.1 (seven loaves)
8.14 (the 13th loaf)

The third five:
8.22 the blind man at Bethsaida
9.14 a man with a deaf and dumb spirit
10.46 blind Bartimaeus
11.15 the cleansing of the Temple
14.22 (the feeding of the disciples)
16.1 Jesus's resurrection

Together, these make three series of five healings, with feedings included among them.

People today wish each other an Easter greeting in the words "Happy Easter." I usually hear it said in a tone of voice that has a slight weariness in it. It is not a joyful weariness of faith, a stake-your-life commitment. I don't think it is just weary from the extra Holy Week services. It is more like a hollow sound, a tone of uncertainty, not really sure that it's all for real. It might be almost cynical, as in "we know what *really* happened."

Remember "Turkey Day"? Those were the words people use for a holiday formerly called "Thanksgiving," when they have no thanks to give, or no-one to give thanks to. The Easter greeting *used* to be, "Christ is Risen!", to which one responded, "Truly he is risen!" Or in Greek, *Christos Anestè, Alethōs anestè*. Now that is faith—but what is it faith *in*?

How did this sad and sorry Easter greeting come about? First, because people simply don't find any literal reading of the Resurrection texts both intelligible and plausible. If the Resurrection were a resuscitation (and Paul says that it was not), then Jesus would have died for real later on, as Lazarus presumably did, after the story in the Gospel of John. The texts pretty clearly have something else in mind. A resuscitation would undermine their message, whatever it is. A resuscitation and later death-for-real would "call off the party." But what is the party about?

If it was some kind of preternatural event, there are other problems. Such an event, if it could make sense, if it could have happened then, is not the sort of thing that happens to us now, and so it doesn't help us much now. It is then irrelevant.

Even worse, such an event is impossible to really know, if it is conceived in naturalistic terms, even if it is conceived as an *exception* to natural laws. For even in "exceptions" to natural laws, the material bodies do something, they move from here to there. They have a trajectory, even if it was the wrong trajectory, even if it was not the trajectory the natural laws said they should have had. But in the Resurrection even that trajectory cannot be specified. It is impossible to say *what happened*, and so it is impossible to know what this "event" was all about. One is left with a "something happened (but I don't know what)." I am supposed to stake my life on this?! Figuring out what is *proposed* for belief in a "literal" Resurrection is already impossible; deciding whether to believe it is then moot.

It would be odd to ask people to stake their lives on something that cannot be spelled out, events that cannot be told or disclosed. And clearly these texts do ask people to stake their lives on something. But what?

The question of the events (if any) behind the Resurrection texts can be left to New Testament scholars. They profess themselves to be uncommonly perplexed by the problem. The theology in the texts is more accessible, and if they are read as advertisements for faith, they do make sense.

I think the Resurrection texts pose a challenge, a question whether limitation can *really* bear blessing, when the limitation is really real, i.e., terminal. If these texts are read as advertisements, they are plain enough, and it is pretty clear what the product is. There is a saying, "you pays your money and you takes your chances." Here, you buy the product or you don't. The product, however, is not really invisible, for one can see exposure, limitation, and need, and one can see the lives of other people who have embraced them and found life more abundantly. It is possible to say, "I want what they have." But such an approach would be to abandon the attempt to find literal readings, on the suspicion that some other reading might make better sense.

It is not just the Resurrection that is at stake; much of the Gospel of Mark is lost if the miracle texts are abandoned. Mark went to a lot of trouble to put these texts in a series, from small miracles to large. They carry much of his meaning, and the structure of the series carries his thesis. The teaching of Jesus carries the same message as the advertisements. He says basically three things: (1) Repent! The Kingdom of Heaven is upon you! I.e, the jig is up, exposure is coming, and it would be a good idea to get ready to embrace it. (2) Stop making invidious comparisons with your neighbors and accept life in gratitude and joy. I.e., limitation is to be embraced just as exposure was. (3) And lastly, love (that is, help) your neighbor in need. These things are clear enough, once someone points them out for you. I heard them from Edward Hobbs.

The "miracles" say, as advertisements do, that the product will actually bring life, life more abundantly. The cleansings are about exposure. This is in part a legacy of the Common Documents, for in Leviticus, skin diseases are a sign of uncleanness, and uncleanness is there a prototype of being in a state of sin. The raisings are about limitation, and the feedings are about need. Jesus cleanses, raises, feeds: he brings new life where before there was only guilt, frustration, and abandonment. It would be odd to dismiss the miracles. If the miracles are ignored, what's the point? If they are read literally, they become advice to *evade* exposure, limitation, and need, and then what happens to the teaching? It would be undermined also.

Why say this in advertisements, rather than "straight" ? It has a certain irony. For we know that exposure can be devastating, limitation in the end kills us all, and the resources spent on other people cannot be spent on myself. The pains are real, and they get us in the end. The irony in these advertisements is essential. For without it, we could not see the human predicament, caught between the pain of the disappointments and the blessing that comes in them. The irony carries a message. It is a way of saying, "We see the pains of life, and we affirm life as good—not just in spite of the pains, but in and through the pains."

This is easily missed. The "miracles" *look* like a fairly common theme in the first century. There were plenty of stories about people who were called "divine men," wandering miracle workers. But the "divine man" got people *out* of limitation, rather than show them the blessing *in* limitation. Exposure and need were silently ignored (and thus evaded just as much as limitation). Mark knows that the Jesus stories were sometimes heard as "divine man" stories, and he allows the reader to mistake the early miracles for just such stories. But he makes it clear where his own heart lies as his Tell unfolds. The disciples consistently misunderstand, they want power, where Mark's Jesus came in weakness, and came to suffer. The disciples want to meet exposure, limitation, and need from a position of power, one where they can control things and be exempted from the pains of life, not submit to them. Jesus had other plans.

Our theme in this book is about misunderstandings of historical religion in naturalistic terms. Naturalistic readings of the miracle texts and of the Resurrection are a case in point. There is more than just innocent misunderstanding here, however. For a naturalistic reading of these stories all but inevitably promotes exemption from limitation, not the embracing of it. And as usual, exposure and need can then be silently ignored.

Remember that the supernatural works as naturalism by other means. Naturalism works here as objectivation, a way to make the good news "objective"—and so relieve the believer of the responsibility for making it "subjective," of making it active in his own life. What a neat trick! It simultaneously gets the believer off the hook, *and* converts the belief from one of finding the good even in the pains of life to just evading the pains of life.

The Resurrection is not about getting out of limitation, it is about finding blessing that comes in limitation. To do that, you don't need biological anomalies. What the theologian doesn't need, the historian is in no position to supply. Remember the Virgin Birth? In "God's Driver's License"? It didn't need biological anomalies, either. Those who want the Resurrection to get them out of death are trying to get out of limitation, not find blessings in it.

Chapter 8

Hot Talk

8.1 Rachel

There is a story in the Common Documents, in Genesis 31.17–42 to be precise, that tells us something about the encounter between nature religions and historical religions. Three thousand years ago, people may have understood the difference better than we do today.

As the story begins, Jacob has long ago cheated his brother Esau out of his birthright at their father Isaac's deathbed. Their mother Rachel sent Jacob out of town to her brother Laban's house both to get him out of the way of Esau's wrath and also to find a wife for him. He found two, Leah and Rachel, and stayed twenty years. His wives and concubines had eleven or twelve children (thirteen, if you count Dinah), and he grew rich, largely by shrewder goat-breeding than Uncle Laban was capable of. Thinking it is time to head home to the land of Canaan while he still can, Jacob packs up family and loot and leaves. And Rachel steals her father Laban's household idols (v. 19).

It takes Laban three days to notice, and he comes storming after them outraged. They were rude enough to leave without saying good-bye, and Oh, by the way, what about the household idols? Lots of these idols have been dug up in excavations in the ancient Near East, usually female fertility goddesses. They are typically a few inches tall, rarely more than a foot, about the size of a TV remote control. Very portable. Jacob for once is exceeded in guile by his junior wife Rachel (it didn't happen often). He invites uncle Laban to search the camp, and whoever is found to have the idols shall die.

Laban doesn't find the idols, of course. When he comes to his daughter Rachel, she has hidden the idols in what the translators call a camel's litter, and she is sitting on it. She says to Daddy, "Daddy, it's that time of the month; you will understand if I can't get up." The editors (or translators?) have been quite discreet. The idols are hiding in a port-a-potty.

This story is in a composite narrative, from what are known as the J and E sources. The encounter about the stolen idols is probably from the E source. Now J and E both are opposed to idols, but they handle the problem very differently from the later D and P sources. D, the "Deuteronomist," breaks out into allergies and seizures at the sight of the smallest idol. Theological alarm of the first order, remedied only by the strongest anathemas. J and E are not panicked, but instead are quite laid back. If the idols have to hide in a port-a-potty, they can't be very powerful.

In the same way, some theologies today have stolen the household idols of naturalistic religion. They have to hide them, and the most convenient place is one that cannot be searched. This is how cause laundering works: it hides acts of God in areas of physics that are closed to inspection, in practice if necessary, in principle if possible. It is very much like hiding the idols in the port-a-potty. These godlets are not very powerful if they have to hide where nobody can see them. And acts of God are not much to sneeze at if they have to hide in a cause-laundry.

J and E had something grander in mind. They envision a God who acts in history but is not an intramundane actor in history. A God who is powerful enough to bring good out of events no matter how events turn out is a God who doesn't need to manipulate events. Naturalism (and cause laundering) presuppose that if good is to be brought out of events, the god will have to manipulate events to make them come out right. The God of history is neither so small nor so limited by events in the world.

Why would some theologies today want to pack off with the household idols of nature religions? Because nature religions manipulate events so the believer doesn't have to put up with the full pains of life. Nature religion works to get people out of the pains, rather than to find blessings in them. And retaining vestiges of nature religion is a good way to have a back-up insurance policy, in case historical-covenantal religion doesn't find enough blessing in the pains of life. Understandable nostalgia, understandable hedging of bets. But a God that is big enough to bring good out of the pains of life doesn't need such maneuvers.

8.2 Maxxianic Consciousness

Our problem has been to show how the believer can be responsible in making claims for faith. It appeared originally in the confusions about the "objective" and the "subjective." It has colored Christian thinking about Jesus for two hundred years.

In the nineteenth century, people began to suspect that the Gospels were not the literal reports they were taken to be. The life of Jesus began to raise more questions than answers. The "miracles" had until then been believed literally, on the assumption that a literal reading was coherent and possible. That assumption failed in the nineteenth century, as it had already failed for some in the eighteenth. Problems multiplied for Christian scholars. Doubts about the "miracles" were just the beginning. As we have noticed already, Mark arranges the miracles in his story to suit his own editorial purposes, which makes it mildly unlikely that the order in the text corresponds to any temporal sequence in actual fact. But that was not noticed until after mid-century. Indeed, much of the century was spent trying to reconstruct a history of Jesus as we would write a history—with events in proper temporal order, after due sifting of witnesses and evidence, etc. In other words, they attempted to write an external history, only to discover that the Gospels are internal histories and provide minimal evidence of the background external history.

This was the time when people discovered that Mark was the first Gospel, a source for Matthew and Luke, rather than an abridgment of Matthew. The first three Gospels follow each other fairly closely in actual wording, in common materials, and in general tone. Even the order of events is the same more often than not. They were regarded as historically more reliable than John. John, the theologian of the bunch, and regarded as historically unreliable, ironically set the theological agenda for the nineteenth and twentieth centuries. The task was to figure out who Jesus was. And the question really was a search for an "objective" answer, something that would relieve the believer of responsibility. If we only knew who he was, we could know whether to believe in him or not. If we only knew who he *thought* he was, etc.

Albert Schweitzer wrote a history of this effort in *The Quest of the Historical Jesus*, in 1906. It was not a celebration, for virtually all of the effort was a failure. Each generation refuted its predecessors without establishing itself safe against its successors. As Ernst Troeltsch observed at about the same time as Schweitzer, people tend to see in history the parts that have analogies in contemporary experience and contemporary values. It came as a sad surprise at the end of the century when someone noticed that Jesus was not a nineteenth-century Liberal.

At the end of the nineteenth century, the Germans, who have more words than we English-speakers do, discovered that they could distinguish between what we have to call the "historical" and the "historic"—in German, the *historische* and the *geschichtliche*. *Historie* is "just the historical facts," where *Geschichte* is the story told from within, showing the meaning, the significance for people now. *Historie* is a bit dry and dull; *Geschichte* is lively. I have made a similar distinction myself, above, but it is one that can be made in many ways. It can be used to evade responsibility and it can be used to embody responsibility. In any case, at the start of the twentieth century, this distinction allowed people a lot of room to play. For it relieved them of the burden of demonstrating what they wanted to find in the (external) historical facts, and they could posit it instead in the (internal) historical significance of events whose factuality need not trouble them too much. Still, if there was a way to hang the significance on the external facts, they wanted to find it. Actually, they wanted to hang the significance on the external facts without taking responsibility for it themselves, as we shall see.

Among theologians, the doctrine of who Jesus was and what he did is called "Christology," the study of the Christ. The loss of the supernatural ruled out one traditional way of doing Christology. With a supernatural, God literally descends into the world and interrupts the ordinary processes of the world. The theological advantage of such a scheme, merits of the supernatural aside, is that it presupposes the divinity that one seeks to "find" in Jesus, and thereby makes that divinity safe from questioning. Such Christologies have been termed Christologies "from above." With the loss of the supernatural, some attempted to reconstruct Christology, but "from below," starting from human experience and the evidence of history. Out of these attempts there sprung many of the questions of twentieth-century Christology. They were for the most part quests for something "objective" that the believer could hang his faith on. When the credibility of these projects wore thin, others returned to Christology from above, but without the supernatural, or with a minimalist supernatural. This was usually limited to just a literal Resurrection, deeply shrouded in obfuscation ("mystery"), and, for Catholics, a literal Virgin Birth (also obfuscated).

Some people tried to objectivate Jesus's divine status by finding it in his own "messianic consciousness." The search for his "messianic consciousness" was a quest for the whatever-it-was about his psychology by which he conceived his own mission and identity. How did he understand himself? Perhaps the messianic titles can tell us, for the New Testament has lots of names for Jesus, some of them quite enigmatic, offering work to keep scholars employed for decades.

It was not noticed that this kind of theology was circular in an unattractive way, for Jesus's sense of who he was could make a difference only if he really were who he thought he was. It is not necessary to resort to comparisons with delusional psychoses today to highlight the circularity and weakness of such an argument. It would be enough to notice that many people are poor judges of their own work. From time to time, most of us are overrated in our own estimation. Who

Jesus thought he was would be acutely difficult to recover, and also not all that convincing even if we could recover it.

What, one may ask, did people hope to gain by Christological projects such as these, the search for messianic consciousness, or the theology in the messianic titles? First and foremost, it gets the believer off the hook. It demonstrates in an "objective" way what the believer is supposed to believe in. And once that demonstration is "out there," the believer can point to it as "evidence." The search for objectivity in Christology allows us to continue the same old game by other means, a modern game, but one in which the faithful still don't have to take responsibility for their faith. The basic human questions never have to be faced, questions about whether exposure, limitation, and need really bear blessings or not.

It is as if there were a sequel to *Thunderdome*, one set many centuries or millennia in the far future, when the Christological parallels of the movie set in the late twentieth century have developed into a religion, one with a long history and origins no longer entirely clear. I don't know whether this fantasy is a farce or a nightmare. But Mad Max is the founder of this religion, or at least he was made such after the events of the original *Thunderdome* movie. The Tell and its derivative stories have come to be interpreted literally, and Mad Max and Captain Walker were long ago identified as one and the same person, a savior who came to rescue the Tribe at the Oasis and lead them out of barrenness and into the promised land (i.e., Sydney). Times change, and the theoreticians of this religion have reinvented critical history, and now doubt the historicity of some of the particulars of the Tell. The central theory is of course about the person and work of Mad Max, and it is called Maxxiology. One imagines a final examination in a Maxxiology course, in these questions:

> Comment on each of the following themes in contemporary Maxxiology:
> 1. Mad Max's maxxianic consciousness.
> 2. The distinction between the historical Max and the historic, biblical Walker (*Der Sogennante historische Max und der geschichtliche, biblische Walker*).

3. Maxxiologies based on the theory of the Maxximal Walker.

4. Mad Max's self-understanding.

5. His Walking Consciousness.

6. Contrasts between Walkerology from above and Maxxiology from below.

7. Comment on the Quest for the historical Max in the Maxxiological literature of a century ago?

8. The New Quest for the historical Max.

9. The Third Quest for the historical Max.

10. The significance of "Raggedy Man" as a Maxxiological title.

11. Evaluate the thesis that Mad Max and Captain Walker were the same, because his real name was Max Walker ("he really *was* Captain Walker").

12. Was there a physical, bodily ascension of the Flying Jalopy?

13. Comment on The Blessed Mrs. Walker in recent Maxxiology.

It would be too simple just to ask, did they really get out OK? Did the Tribe get to where they wanted to? Did they find life more abundantly, if the New Testament allusion is not too pompous?

In the same way, one could ask about the New Testament, do exposure, limitation and need really bear blessing? Or are they barren? Was saving exposure incarnate in Jesus? Or not? Does it make sense to embrace exposure as gracious, limitation as opportunity for creativity, and need as opening to community and fellowship? Do they really bring life more abundantly?

The New Testament does give us a little evidence for an "external" history, the "just the facts" history. In Hans Conzelmann's minimalist appraisal (1973), we can have some confidence that he grew up in Nazareth, was baptized by John the Baptist, and was crucified on a cross. There is not much else. These events either do not fulfill prophecies from the Common Documents or (in the case of the baptism) are an embarrassment to the evangelists. All else is arranged

for purposes of each evangelist's Tell. The narrative order is constructive and theological, rather than historical. The teaching must have
some traditional elements in it, but there is much in the teaching that
only makes sense in the context of the church later in the first century. Sorting out which is which is not always easy. The events have
been turned into advertisements for faith. In the end, that is what the
Gospels are about: invitations to faith, a certain kind of faith. It is very
much like the great Deuteronomic sermons, of which the one at the
end of Joshua is exemplary. Joshua asks and challenges the assembled
Israelites, "Choose this day, which gods you will serve. As for me and
mine, we will serve the Lord." So what are you gonna do, when faced
with exposure, limitation, and need?

Living in a world-affirming historical religion is like that. There is
no proof, nothing "objective" that could get the believer off the hook.
And the scoffers will always jeer, when things are going badly, when
the blessings in exposure, limitation and need are nowhere to be seen,
"Where, now, O Israel, is your God?" To that there is no answer except
to live covenantally.

8.3   Darmok at Tanagra

In the last quarter of the twentieth century there were several television
series called "Star Trek." They frequently undertook philosophical issues in their plots, sometimes posing questions of popular philosophical interest, sometimes posing "what-if" scenarios that were quite
imaginative. In one of them, the captain of the Enterprise, Jean-Luc
Picard, finds himself in the El'A'Dral system, trying to communicate
with Tamarians, a race deemed incomprehensible from previous en-
counters. The words make sense, but their meaning does not. The
captain of the Tamarian vessel says something about "Darmok and
Jilad at Tanagra," and then he and Picard meet on the surface of one
of the planets in the system. Picard and Dathon, the Tamarian captain,
have no better luck communicating on the surface of the planet than
they did by radio, ship-to-ship. Picard's first assumption is that he has
been challenged to single combat, a duel. He refuses. Dathon replies

in frustration, "Chaka, when the walls fell." Meanwhile, the crew of the Enterprise is trying to research the puzzle, and discovers that there is a Darmok, a mythical figure associated with a mythical place called Tanagra, in the legends of one of the thousands of systems known to their computer library.

Picard and Dathon are assaulted by an unknown scintillating shape. Picard makes an intuitive leap, and guesses that the Tamarians communicate solely by metaphor. Dathon replies in elation, "Sokath, his eyes uncovered!" The guess is correct. Correct but, little help, because the human crew of the Enterprise still does not know the history that the references to Darmok or Chaka or Sokath rely upon. The plot of the story winds to its end without anything more of philosophical interest happening.

A reviewer was surprised: "Now *this* was an intriguing idea, no doubt about it. I find the concept of a race which communicates only via imagery and metaphor a fascinating one, and that portion of it was extremely well done and well executed" (Lynch, 1994). Evidently the reviewer is not familiar with this kind of thinking. But it happens all the time. A prime example is Monty Python's *The Life of Brian*, a movie in which one Brian of Nazareth grows up in the time of Jesus and comes to a similar end, but without the holy water and hagiography. Brian is just an ordinary joe, caught up in the currents of his time, trying to survive and in the end crucified among thirty-odd other felons. Monty Python's comedy really makes sense only if you are familiar with the Gospel narratives of the life of Jesus.

For some, the movie must have seemed sacrilegious, mocking everything that is sacred in the Gospels. But the theme of the movie seems to be that Brian, at least, whatever may be said of Jesus, came in weakness, and came to suffer. (Jesus puts in a cameo appearance at the beginning of the movie, and clearly is an object of veneration in the warm and radiant glow of sanctity even at birth. He is not heard from again.) Actually, the idea of coming in weakness and suffering is the theme of the Gospel of Mark, an idea that we saw in the miracle sequence in Mark. Three times, in the middle of chapters eight, nine, and ten, Mark has Jesus announce that he came in weakness, to suffer.

Monty Python's *Life of Brian* is offensive to those for whom Jesus has become shrouded in an odor of sanctity that has hidden the original message. It is offensive because *Brian* makes Mark's message clear, clear enough to speak for itself, even if they are deaf to it in Mark's text, and they don't like it.

What may come as a surprise is that the Gospel stories *themselves* are written much the way Monty Python's script was written: as a take-off, a parody. They are a parody of the Exodus, incomplete in Mark, filled out in Matthew and Luke. The key to the parallel is that for the Gospel writers and readers, Jesus is the new Israel, the one who leads Israel into the promised land again. Remember that Jacob and his sons went down into Egypt (the short historical creed, "My father was a wandering Aramaean ... " ?), and there became a great and mighty nation. Moses, the one who was to lead them out of Egypt, was born after the Pharaoh ordered the slaughter of all the Hebrew male babies. They came out through the desert, were fed by angels, and eventually crossed the Jordan river at Jericho and entered the promised land from the east. After some time of settlement, David, then their leader, captures the city of Jerusalem and makes it his capital. Here are the parallels: Joseph and Mary are warned to flee Herod's wrath in Egypt. Herod slaughters all the baby boys in Bethlehem. Jesus is tempted (tested) in the wilderness by Satan, and fed by angels. He crosses the Jordan at Jericho at the beginning of his ministry. After his ministry, he, too, goes up to Jerusalem. In other words, both Israels start in the land of Canaan, both leave Egypt in circumstances associated with a slaughter of innocents, both are tested and fed in the desert, both cross the Jordan at Jericho, and both eventually go up to Jerusalem, one in a simple triumph, the other in a very ironic "triumph."

The evangelists trusted that their readers would recognize the Exodus story retold, as the Tamarians would recognize the parallels with Darmok at Tanagra. We the viewers, by the way, never find out the original story of Darmok at Tanagra, and so with respect to Star Trek we are very much in the same position as most readers of the Gospels today, who do not recognize the parody of the Exodus.

The parallels in the plot are not the only ones in the Gospels.

Remember that there were a baker's dozen of tribes in the canonical
list for Israel; twelve that had land, and the Levites, priests without
any land of their own. Now the number thirteen in the Gospel of
Mark makes sense: it is always called twelve, but careful counting
always finds thirteen. (Disciples, for only one more example.) The
twelve (thirteen) are Israel, whatever is thirteen is the new Israel. Jesus
cleanses and raises and feeds the new Israel. At least that's what the
writer of Mark intended.

Where to go from here? First, thinking in history is not as simple as
it had appeared. Narratives get much of their meaning from parallels
with other narratives. We saw this long ago in fiction, in the three
movies set in the south Pacific or near it in Australia. Somehow, we
never expected to find it in real history as well.

And second, these texts are saying something about Jesus that
people have mostly missed until recently. Two things, in fact: the bit
about coming in weakness, in the power of weakness; and the parallels
with the Exodus. We have seen both in the last few sections, though
without any mention of Jesus. For the Exodus was the watershed in the
history of religions, the move from world-affirming nature religion to
world-affirming historical religion. And the price of affirming human
life in history is the affirmation also of its hard and painful parts,
exposure, limitation, and need.

There is a fifty-dollar word for this kind of thinking in parallels
in history. It is called "typology." (The earlier event in the parallel is
called the *antetype*, and the later event is called the *antitype*. The two
words are very confusing, differing only by one letter.) More to the
point is the question why does typology challenge its hearers so much
more when both events are real? In *The Life of Brian*, the earlier events
are real, the later ones are fiction, a satire. Monty Python challenges
us well enough in our reading of the Gospels, but more is possible.

When both events in a typological parallel are real, those who
live in the aftermath of the later events are challenged to see them in
the light of the earlier events. When the hearers' lives are directly
impacted, the challenge is escalated. When the earlier events are real
and not fictional or mythical or legendary, they escalate the challenge

further. For the reality of the past events gives them their challenge: they *demonstrate* that what happened then is possible now. It is not merely hypothetical; it has happened before. (This is what history does instead of scientific objectivity: history demonstrates what is possible in human life.)

These parallels in the Gospels present a challenge that is all too often missed today. They should demonstrate by their invocation of the Exodus that world-affirming historical religion is still possible. (For some, this was in doubt after 70 CE, the year the Romans destroyed the Temple in Jerusalem.) And they show how the engagement with the pains of history in the Exodus can be continued after the disasters that came to first-century Judaism.

The Rabbis also engage in typology, just as much as Christians do; Exodus typology in particular. One need only consult Mark Podwal's Passover Haggadah. The text is traditional and fixed, but the illustrations are at the liberty of the book designer. They show the parallels between the Exodus from Egypt and the return from the Babylonian Exile, later Jewish exoduses from Czarist oppression, the Spanish Inquisition, the Nazis, and the Soviets. Christians have no monopoly on Exodus typology.

That, by the way, shows that there are always more ways than just one to draw parallels in history. We shall come to this point at length below, but one thing may be observed here. In our original dilemma, there was more than met the eye. We thought it was a forced choice between science and religion. On further exploration, a recurrent theme showed itself, badly described as a choice between "objectivity" and "subjectivity." The objective is "out there," and the subjective is "just" inside of me. More important and less obvious is the feature that the "objective" excuses me from responsibility. At least it does in naturalistic settings, where the questions are about what happens in nature. The "subjective" supposedly cannot be justified, and cannot challenge other people, because it is something that is just made-up, caprice or whimsy or wishful thinking. At least this is the case in naturalistic settings, where the questions are about what happens in nature.

History is different from nature. The really real cannot just be defined to be the objective. We saw that already with the kid cruising on a summer evening. What he is doing is not in the least settled merely by appeal to the motions of any of the bodies involved, his own, the automobile's, or any other. For such a question about the motions of bodies presupposes a prior selection of *which* bodies to ask about. Do we include the people at home? The other kids who are also out on this summer evening? It hardly makes sense to claim that the answer to our original question (what is this kid *doing?*) is "just" subjective. He really was going to the store for bread and milk, or cruising, or recharging the battery, etc. And some possible answers really can be ruled out, depending on the surrounding circumstances. Nevertheless, the choice of what circumstances to include is made by those who tell the story, and is not determined by the motions of any of the bodies themselves.

So how is it that history challenges, that history can speak truth in ways that the language of the sciences cannot? Beyond the range and the reach of scientific language, the language of nature? Typology is an example. In the twentieth century, after the Holocaust, things look different. Attempts at "ethnic cleansing," especially in Europe, attempts that might or might not have been deplored but certainly would have been tolerated in earlier centuries, are no longer tolerable. They look different now than they would have in the nineteenth century. More generally, Christian attitudes toward Rabbinic Judaism look different after the Holocaust. It would be absurd to dismiss such changes as "just" subjective. But they are clearly not "objective" in the sense of objectivity in the sciences, either. They are the work of typology, and typology does speak a kind of truth, if one different from the language of differential equations and physics. Perhaps the best we can say is that a good typology challenges and speaks truth, a weak one fails to challenge, and a bad one can mislead.

Chapter 9

Your Move

9.1 How to Clean an Oven

Our constant theme has been objectivity and subjectivity in naturalistic questions, and the appearance that one is caught in a dilemma between them in history. Instead, responsibility is what people do in history. The spectre of subjectivity has nevertheless loomed over life in history. I would like to sharpen that apparent threat, though not to induce abject panic in the reader. Again and again we have come against the question whether the pains of life bring blessings or instead are barren. The believer was left without visible means of support except the testimony of lives lived trusting in such blessing.

It gets worse. There are more ways than just one to do that.

The Talmud is a collection of writings dating from the second century of the Common Era to perhaps the sixth or eighth. The core of it is the Mishnah, a collection intermediate in size between the Common Documents and the New Testament; not very big. The commentary on the Mishnah, called the Gemara, is much bigger. Together, they are the size of a small encyclopedia. It has been the shaper of Rabbinic Judaism, the general instructions for how to continue after the loss of the Temple in 70 CE.

There is a story in the Talmud, a dispute about how to clean an oven. Rabbi Eliezer ben Hyrcanus is on one side of the dispute, and

Rabbi Joshua (and all the other rabbis) are on the other side of the dispute. Eliezer is in a minority of one. The particulars of cleaning the oven don't matter.

The story makes many points along the way, and perhaps the simplest thing is to note them as it moves along. (The story is in Baba Meẓi'a, folio 59b, pp. 154–155 in the Neusner translation.) Eliezer marshals every conceivable argument, to no avail. So he says to the others, "If the law accords with my position, this carob tree will prove it. The carob tree was uprooted from its place by a hundred cubits—and some say, four hundred cubits." The other rabbis are unimpressed. Eliezer tries again. He appeals to a stream of water. It flows backwards. They are unimpressed. He says that if he is right, the walls of the schoolhouse are to fall down. The walls totter. The rabbis are unimpressed. Rabbi Joshua tells the walls to butt out, and they stop at a forty-five degree angle, torn between respect for one rabbi and respect for the other. (All this, by the way, is a misguided attempt to find answers in nature for an essentially historical problem, precisely the mistake we want to escape from in this book.)

Then Eliezer appeals to Heaven. A voice from Heaven says, "What business have you with R. Eliezer, for the law accords with his position under all circumstances!" But Rabbi Joshua retorted, "It is not in heaven (Dt. 30.12)." What comes next seems odd to our ears: the Torah is given on earth, and so it is wrong to appeal to Heaven. "After the majority you are to incline."

This is a strong statement. It is also surprising—and so it needs emphasis of the clearest sort. Rabbi Nathan asks Elijah what God thought of these proceedings. "What did the Holy One, blessed be He, do at that moment?" Elijah replied that God laughed with joy, and said, "My children have overcome me, my children have overcome me!" (Baba Meẓi'a, folio 59b, Babylonian Talmud vol. 21B, pp. 154–155, Neusner trans.). Human religious communities have the authority to dispose of their own affairs. God agrees, even when he doesn't agree.

The English translation continues to the effect that the rabbis took a vote and excommunicated Rabbi Eliezer. The footnote in the Soncino translation says that the text in the original actually reads that they "blessed" him—and that blessed here means excommunicated. This story serves multiple purposes. There is more here than just a grant of discretionary authority to human congregations, though that is the most obvious point. It is also in the New Testament, for those who care, in the words "what you bind on earth is bound in heaven," etc., in "It seemed good to the Holy Spirit and to us," and in "the liberty wherewith Christ hath made us free." (Matthew 18.18, Acts 15.28, Galatians 5.1). The principle is the same.

But back to the footnote. The passage in the Mishnah that this story comments on and illustrates is as follows:

> Just as a claim of fraud applies in buying and selling, so a claim of fraud applies to spoken words. One may not say to [a storekeeper], "How much is this object?" knowing that he does not want to buy it. If there was a penitent, one may not say to him, "Remember what you used to do." If he was a child of proselytes, one may not say to him, "remember what your folks used to do!" For it is said, And a proselyte you shall not wrong nor oppress (Ex. 22.20). (Baba Meẓiʿa 4.10, vol. 21B, p. 151, Neusner trans.).

It is not just an injunction to be fair in transactions, but more generally, an injunction to tact and forbearance with other people all the time.

The conclusion that I would like to draw can be sketched only in outline, but the reader is entitled to know what is involved in conducting a world-affirming historical religion. There are more ways than just one to conduct a covenant. There were more ways than just two in Judaism of the first century, though only two survived. One became the orthodox Judaism of the Synagogue, the other became the Church. There is (and was) a responsible liberty of interpretation in the conduct of a covenant. I would rather not repeat the sorry history of how this principle has been rejected on both sides by the Church and the Synagogue subsequent to their birth out of the disasters of the first century. (This is in a dull work called *Elementary Monotheism*.)

Instead, it is enough to observe the fatal mistake. It was the assumption, made on both sides, that only one daughter religion could legitimately inherit from the ashes of Second Temple Judaism. Each had its apologetic strategies for disinheriting the other.

I would like to suggest a different approach. From the point of view of the Church (from which, if not for which, I can speak), the existence of another Exodus tradition is living witness to one's own responsible liberty of interpretation in the conduct of a covenant. The mere existence of the other Exodus tradition makes it obvious that to continue the tradition at all is an act of interpretation, and one for which human interpreters are obliged to take responsibility. We return to the issue we began with, the choice between objectivity and subjectivity, or responsibility in history. Some things can be observed at this point.

The existence of the other tradition is an instance of *exposure*, albeit not exposure of sin. It is exposure of responsibility, and that can be painful enough, simply because it creates a real anxiety for members of the exposed tradition. In other words, you can't get away with thinking that God made your religion, but other people invented their religions. You're just like the other people, you invented your own religion. What is said for the Church can be mirrored with some changes for the Synagogue. But exposure is exposure, and we are committed, if the reader is with me so far, to embracing exposure as something that brings grace and freedom. Because the existence of another Exodus tradition is exposure, Christianity needs Rabbinic Judaism to be strong, healthy, and different. Continuing Judaism with the rabbis in the Synagogue is part of the liberty wherewith Christ hath made us *all* free, and Christians should respect that freedom.

9.2   No Shadow or Turning

So it appears as if life in history has more difficulties than just the pains of history. It is impossible to know what happened, because the interpretation of human actions is always open. It is impossible to know how to continue a covenant into the future. In fact, you can make up a covenant any way you like!

Or so it appears.

Naturalism has unambiguous answers to all questions, or at least to all the questions that it can see. There are no uncertainties, things are objective. And from the perspective of naturalism, thinking in historical terms is hopelessly subjective.

Things appear differently from the perspective of one who understands history. Naturalistic thinking makes "objective" things that are in fact human choices, the results of human interpretation. And objectivation relieves the human interpreter of responsibility. The entire project of locating acts of God in particular physical events, and calling those events the causal part of the acts of God is a case in point, and it is the example with which we started this book. Once the acts of God are objectivated (here, in quantum indeterminacy), the human acts by which they are ascribed to events are hidden, covered up. The act of interpretation is also an act of faith, and once hidden, the believer is off the hook, and doesn't have to take responsibility for it. But we saw two drawbacks in this project. Objectivation in physical indeterminacy always involves cause laundering, and there is no way to tell which quantum fluctuations are acts of God and which ones are just quantum fluctuations. From the perspective of naturalism, that decision is hopelessly subjective, and the proponents of naturalistic theology hoped we wouldn't notice. So on its own terms, the naturalistic project of locating acts of God in particular events *as delineated by physical theory* has problems with no prospect of easy solution.

Responsibility from the point of view of history is something different from the dilemma of objectivity and subjectivity. We have already seen that the question of what a *human* act is does not have any answer from naturalistic resources alone. Nature may rule out some answers, but it can never settle the question of which narrative the act is to be fitted into, and that narrative placement determines the act "from outside" more than any of the physical particulars of the act can. Ultimately, history itself is needed as the narrative context for making sense of human actions, even small ones. Religious language of acts of God is open also; nature could never determine what an act of God is, even when acts of God have an undeniably material substrate, as in the parting of the Sea of Reeds.

The easiest way to retrace our steps, if we are to make sense of acts of God, is to look at the disappointments of life. If one would live open-eyed in history, they must be faced. We sorted them out into three kinds, exposure, limitation, and need. In a world-affirming historical religion, the believing soul responds to each in acts that presuppose trust in some kind of blessing brought in each disappointment. One could ask for "objective" proof that they bring blessings, but there is none. The question of responsibility gets posed differently. We each make our own answers to the questions posed in exposure, limitation, and need. And while there is no "objective" (i.e., naturalistic) guide to the "right" answers, we shall be compared with those who found good and blessings, at great cost to themselves, where others saw life as only barren and defective. It is that comparison that exposes, and it is that comparison that is rejected by those who reject the pains of life as barren. That comparison says all that needs to be said, more than any proof or derivation could.

One may ask, however, in a philosophical vein, *whether* people are right to embrace the pains of life as good-bearing, without thereby asking for proof. Peter Berger once posed the question in the form of the comfort that a mother gives to a child who has awakened from a nightmare. He asked, in *A Rumor of Angels* (1990), whether the mother who comforts her child with the words, "Everything's OK" is telling the truth or not. Is the mother lying? Is everything all right? *Everything*?! Will the child be OK? How can the mother know? What can she do, in face of all that can go wrong? What on earth could the mother really mean? She knows that a bus could hit the child, and then it's *not* all right.

So what can we say stands behind the faith that it is "all right"? That the pains of life bear blessing? It is not something within the world. It is not something "outside" the world, because the world could then just be extended to include that thing that was formerly outside of it. Perhaps we could just borrow the vernacular, and say, "That's The Way Things Are." That's what people say when they get tired of you pestering them and asking "why?" questions without end. The Way Things Are is not a thing in the world, nor is it outside the world. It is not a feature of the world, though it is immanently present in the world.

Such language can doubtless be abused as much as the older language of God can. Let other people break it, as they surely will, in time. Look at how it works. "The Way Things Are" does not interfere with nature or natural processes, yet it shows itself in nature and history without being a cause in nature or an actor in history. It is not a part of the world set off from other parts of the world. Where naturalistic theology has to think of divine acts as set off from other parts of physical causation, "The Way Things Are" does not. It is not a thing, that might or might not exist. It is not outside the world in a way that could be roped into the world. It is not outside the world in a way that would leave the world bereft or abandoned.

Yet it is transcendent, for it escapes any power of language to capture it. We know it by the ways it shows itself in history, bearing blessing in the critical events of history. Language of such a transcendent is always analogical and analogy is always helpless against the scoffer who would say, "Those are *your* analogies." Not as harsh as the "Where, now, O Israel, is your God?" of the Common Documents, but the point is much the same. Indeed, the question just *how*, really, are things? is one that cannot be settled by arguments.

There is a certain confidence here that the reader will understand how the language works. It is like humor more than it is like the language of science. The hearer may get it—and may not. Its consequences are in a way to live, not in something a scientist could measure. One acknowledges the truth of a joke by laughing, but a treatise on the subject-matter of the joke can work to deny its truth. One acknowledges the truth of covenantal stories by living according to them. Theory is necessary, but it is incidental. Theory is supposed to be like street-signs, to tell you where you are in life. When the language of covenant is taken too literally, it works to bring the believer back into nature religion. That's what happens when analogies are taken literally.

Why the personal analogies in meeting the blessings of life, some painful, some joyous? How does the experience of simple joy bestowed by another person shed light on the experience of joy that just comes, without another actor within the world to bestow it? How does the experience of blessing brought in exposure, limitation, and need in the encounter with other human beings shed light on the experience of being exposed, limited, and needed when you are trying to make sense of life as a whole? When we see one part of life in the light of another, we see by analogy. This analogy, the analogy of the personal, is the analogy by which we speak of ultimate reality, the "That's The Way Things Are," as the source and author of exposure, limitation, and need, and of the blessings that come in them. Such an analogy can be twisted in many ways by those who would bend it to purposes other than affirming all of human life as good. And it can be rejected outright, leaving those who speak in this way with no reply that I can see other than to live according to their own analogies.

Yet analogy is always subject to another kind of attack, from its friends, rather than its enemies. Its enemies will simply reject it. Those with more guile will subvert it. Its friends can try to literalize it. The last possibility is the most interesting for us, for literal readings of analogies lead back to objectivation, and from objectivation to naturalism in theology.

Immanuel Kant found the way out of objectivation late in the eighteenth century. Kant is not particularly easy to read, nor is he the latest stage on the road that led through history to an appreciation of human interpretation in making sense of life. Still, Kant marks a kind of watershed, for some theologians take him in stride, and others resist even today. Yet to complain that Kant and his heirs provide cold comfort is to be like the Israelites in the Sinai, who complained, "were there not graves enough in Egypt, that you brought us out here to die?" (Is Kant a desert? Don't believe me; read him yourself.) But the point of the desert is not to live in it, but to get through it.

To ask whether the God who acts "really" acts, at least in everyday language, is to load the word "really" with a very naturalistic freight. To demand that God "really" act in a way describable in the language of physics is to ask to return to Egypt, to return to naturalistic theology.

The Exodus was an exodus not just from Egypt, but also from naturalistic religion, an exodus into history. Through the desert of

Kant lies the land of history, the realm of human responsibility, where nature is of limited help in settling questions. It is no wonder that people cry, "were there not problems enough with naturalism, that you brought us out here into history to die?" Still, the light of history tells what is happening, for those who will hear.

For Further Reading

There are many places where one could begin to read. Most of what follows are merely books and articles that were cited in the text above. But if you were to look for a general or systematic place to begin, you could do very well to start with Merold Westphal's book. Then read Eliade.

Berger, Peter, 1990. *A Rumor of Angels*. New York: Doubleday, 1990.

Bonhoeffer, 1971. *Letters and Papers from Prison; The Enlarged Edition*. Ed. Eberhard Bethge. New York: Macmillan, 1971. Cf. esp. p. 311.

Burns, R. M., 1981. *The Great Debate on Miracles; from Joseph Glanvill to David Hume*. Lewisburg: Bucknell University Press, 1981. I was not convinced by his constructive position at the end, but most of the book is history, well told and fascinating, the story of the first modern theological naturalism in the seventeenth and eighteenth centuries.

Conzelmann, Hans, 1973. *Jesus*. Philadelphia: Fortress Press, 1973.

Eliade, Mircea, 1949. *The Myth of the Eternal Return; or Cosmos and History*. Princeton: Princeton University Press, 1971. The French original was published in 1949. This book is one of the clearest expositions of the differences between nature and history.

Fingarette, Herbert, 1967. *On Responsibility.* New York: Basic Books.

Fingarette, Herbert, 1969. *Self-Deception.* London: RKP: 1969. The central chapters explain the skill of spelling out what is going on in human actions, the problem that we encountered here in the end of chapter 2.

Friedman, Richard Elliott, 1989. *Who Wrote The Bible?.* New York: Harper and Row, 1989.

Hayes, Terry, and George Miller, 1985. *Mad Max—Beyond Thunderdome,* novelized by Joan D. Vinge. New York: Warner Books, 1985.

Heinlein, Robert, 1987. *Stranger in a Strange Land.* New York: Ace Books, 1987.

Hobbs, Edward Craig, 1970. "An Alternate Model from a Theological Perspective." In Herbert A. Otto, *The Family in Search of a Future.* New York: Appleton-Century-Crofts, 1970.

Hobbs, Edward Craig, 1973. "Pluralism in the Biblical Context," Pacific Coast Theological Society, Berkeley, CA., 1973. http://www.pcts.org/pluralism.html.

Hobbs, Edward Craig, 1974. "Gospel Miracle Story and Modern Miracle Stories." In *Gospel Studies in Honor of Sherman Elbridge Johnson,* ed. Massey H. Shepherd Jr. and Edward C. Hobbs. *Anglican Theological Review* Supplemental Series, Number Three, March 1974.

Harvey, Van Austin, 1966. *The Historian and The Believer.* New York: Macmillan, 1966.

Lynch, Timothy, 1994. Synopsis and review of Darmok at Tanagra, episode 102 of Star Trek: The Next Generation. http://www.ugcs.caltech.edu/%7Ewerdna/sttng/tlynch/darmok .rev.html.

MacIntyre, Alasdair, 1988. *Whose Justice? Which Rationality?* University of Notre Dame Press, 1988. MacIntyre explains how one proceeds rationally in an encounter between competing traditions when a neutral judgement standpoint is impossible.

Murray, John Courtney, 1964. *The Problem of God.* Yale University Press, 1964.

Niebuhr, H. Richard, 1970. *Radical Monotheism and Western Culture; With Supplementary Essays.* New York: Harper and Row, 1970.

Niebuhr, H. Richard, 1940. *The Meaning of Revelation.* New York: Macmillan, 1940. This is a somewhat technical and very Neo-Kantian exposition of what it means to be a community that makes sense of its life in terms of history.

Niebuhr, H. Richard, 1963. *The Responsible Self.* New York: Harper and Row, 1963.

Nof, Doron, and Nathan Paldor, 1992. "Are There Oceanographic Explanations for the Israelites' Crossing of the Red Sea?" *Bull. Amer. Meteorological Soc.* 73 no. 3 (1992/03) 305–314.

Placher, William C., 1996. *The Domestication of Transcendence: How Modern Thinking About God Went Wrong.* Louisville, KY: Westminster John Knox Press, 1996.

Podwal, Mark, 1972. *Let My People Go; A Haggadah,* New York: Macmillan, 1972.

Pollard, William G., 1958. *Chance and Providence; God's Action In a World Governed by Scientific Law.* New York: Scribners, 1958.

Porter, Andrew P., and Edward C. Hobbs, 1999. "The Trinity and the Indo-European Tripartite Worldview," *Budhi* (Manila) vol. 3, nos. 2&3 (1999) 1-28. Available on-line at www.jedp.com. This is a short and somewhat technical exposition of the thesis about exposure, limitation, and need. The writing is mine, but the thesis is Edward Hobbs's.

Porter, Andrew P., 2001. *Elementary Monotheism.* 2 vols. Lanham Maryland: University Press of America, 2001. This is technical, and not exhaustive, but it has a lot of detail that is impossible in the present book.

Porter, Andrew P., ca. 2002. *Unwelcome Good News.* In preparation with the present volume. This is a non-technical expansion of the ideas in section 7.1, about exposure, limitation, and need, and how, in the labor of faith, they bring blessings in life.

Rubenstein, Richard L., 1992. *After Auschwitz; History, Theology, and Contemporary Judaism.* 2nd ed. Baltimore: Johns Hopkins University Press, 1992.

Russell, Robert John, 1997. "Does 'The God Who Acts' Really Act?" *Theology Today* 54 no. 1 (1997) 43.

Russell, Robert John, Nancey Murphy, Arthur R. Peacocke, eds., 1995. *Chaos and Complexity; Scientific Perspectives on Divine Action.* Vatican Observatory and the Center for Theology and the Natural Sciences: Notre Dame University Press, 1995.

Sokolowski, Robert, 1982. *The God of Faith and Reason.* Notre Dame: University of Notre Dame Press, 1982.

The Talmud of Babylonia; An American Translation. Translated by Jacob Neusner. Atlanta: Scholars Press, 1990.

Von Rad, Gerhard, 1984. "The Form Critical Problem of the Hexateuch." In *The Problem of the Hexateuch and Other Essays.* London: SCM. Originally published in German in 1938.

Weeden, Theodore J. *Mark: Traditions in Conflict.* Philadelphia: Fortress Press, 1971. This is the long exposition of the thesis that Jesus came in weakness, and the disciples just wanted power. There was an earlier and shorter version (in English) in the *Zeitschrift für die Neutestamentliche Wissenschaft* in 1968.

Westphal, Merold, 1984. *God, Guilt and Death; An Existential Phenomenology of Religion.* Bloomington: Indiana University Press, 1984. The last three chapters are the best.